CORREGIDOR
Siege and Liberation 1941-1945

CORREGIDOR
SIEGE AND LIBERATION 1941-1945

JOHN GREHAN
AND
ALEXANDER NICHOLL

Frontline Books

CORREGIDOR
Siege and Liberation 1941-1945

First published in Great Britain in 2021 by Frontline Books,
an imprint of Pen & Sword Books Ltd,
Yorkshire – Philadelphia

Typeset in 9.5/12.5 Avenir by Dave Cassan.
Printed and bound by CPI Group (UK) Ltd, Croydon, CR0 4YY

Pen & Sword Books Ltd incorporates the imprints of Air World Books, Pen & Sword Archaeology, Atlas, Aviation, Battleground, Discovery, Family History, History, Maritime, Military, Naval, Politics, Social History, Transport, True Crime, Claymore Press, Frontline Books, Praetorian Press, Seaforth Publishing and White Owl.

For a complete list of Pen & Sword titles please contact:

PEN & SWORD BOOKS LTD
47 Church Street, Barnsley, South Yorkshire, S70 2AS, UK.
E-mail: enquiries@pen-and-sword.co.uk
Website: www.pen-and-sword.co.uk

Or

PEN AND SWORD BOOKS,
1950 Lawrence Road, Havertown, PA 19083, USA
E-mail: Uspen-and-sword@casematepublishers.com
Website: www.penandswordbooks.com

CONTENTS

ACKNOWLEDGEMENTS

The authors and publisher would like to extend their grateful thanks, in no particular order, to the following individuals and organisations for their assistance with the images used in this publication: Robert Mitchell, James Luto, Historic Military Press, US Naval History and Heritage Command, US National Museum of Naval Aviation, National Archives and Records Administration, National Museum of the US Air Force, United States Air Force, US Navy, US Library of Congress, United States Marine Corps, USMC Archives, US Army, US War Department, and the US Air Force Historical Support Division.

INTRODUCTION

The Philippine Islands came under US control in May 1898, when they were seized from Spain after an American victory in Manila Bay during the Spanish-American War. Formal title to the islands was granted to the United States by the Treaty of Paris in December of that year.

That the conquest of the Philippines had long been an ambition of the Japanese was a reality that America was well aware of. Consequently, the islands had been placed under the military command of General Douglas MacArthur, who was designated commander of the United States Armed Forces in the Asia-Pacific region. Under him was Major General Lewis R. Brereton, who was in charge of the Far East Air Force.[1] There could be no doubt in either generals' mind that the Philippines would be one of Japan's primary targets.

Above: The invasion of the Philippines underway. This image shows Japanese troops landing at Lingayen Gulf, on the northeast coast of Luzon Island, on 22 December 1941. These landings constituted the main element of the Japanese invasion of the Philippines. (USNHHC)

Above: A Japanese sailor or soldier watches the progress of the landings at Lingayen Gulf on 22 December 1941. (USNHHC)

The US commanders' concerns intensified when Japanese aircraft were spotted probing Philippine air space repeatedly in early December 1941. Any remaining uncertainty as to the enemy's intentions was dispelled when the first news of the devastating attack on Pearl Harbor reached the Philippines.

It was five days before the Japanese made their move against the archipelago. They finally struck on 12 December 1941, when the Japanese 14th Army, under the command of Lieutenant General Masaharu Homma, began occupying Bataan Island off the northern coast of Luzon. The first landings on Luzon itself, the largest and most populous island in the Philippines, took place soon after. Ten days later the main Japanese amphibious assault was delivered against the north of Luzon, targeting the area of Lingayen Gulf with its proximity to the Philippine capital.

Covered by gunfire from cruisers and destroyers, the Japanese troops allocated to the first waves to go ashore at Lingayen Gulf began climbing into their landing craft at 02.00 hours on 22 December. By 04.30 hours, two battalions of the 47th Infantry and one battalion of the 48th Mountain Artillery were in their landing craft, ready to head for their landing beaches. At 05.17 hours the first invaders touched down on the beach south of Agoo Municipality.

'The transfer of the troops to the landing craft had proved extremely difficult because of high seas,' noted the official US historian Louis Morton. 'The light craft were heavily buffeted on the way to shore and the men and equipment soaked by the spray. The radios were made useless by salt water, and there was no communication with the first waves ashore. Even ship-to-ship

Above: With the landings at Lingayen Gulf unopposed, Japanese troops quickly built up supplies and stores ashore, though a number of units had hit the beach in the wrong place. (USNHHC)

communication was inadequate. The men had a difficult time in the heavy surf, and it proved impossible to land heavy equipment. The high seas threw many of the landing craft up on the beach, overturning some and beaching others so firmly that they could not be put back into operation for a full day…

'The second wave could not land as planned, with the result that the entire landing schedule was disrupted. The infantry, mountain artillery, and some of the armor got ashore during the day, but few of the heavy units required for support were able to land.'[2]

Nevertheless, the Japanese were ashore. MacArthur, in direct contradiction of the official American policy of War Plan Orange 3, had chosen to try and stop the enemy on the beaches. With an island the size of Luzon, this was utterly impracticable. Consequently, despite the poor weather, General Homma was able to get the bulk of his forces ashore at Lingayen Gulf with little opposition. In just a few days Japanese troops had secured the northern approaches to Manila.

In the face of the Japanese advance, the US Navy's surface warships and submarine forces were withdrawn to the relative safety of Australia and, with no prospect of any help from the Pacific Fleet at Pearl Harbor, MacArthur finally adopted War Plan Orange 3. This was for the US and Filipino troops to withdraw to defensive positions on the Bataan Peninsula in the hope that they could hold out there until relieved by reinforcements.

Homma urged his men on, with the result that the first attacks were delivered by the Japanese against Bataan on 9 January 1942. By this stage of the fighting in the Philippines only the Bataan

Peninsula and the fortified islands which guarded the entrance to Manila Bay still remained in American hands.

Facing incessant waves of Japanese attacks, over the weeks that followed the defenders on Bataan were gradually pushed back. By the evening of 8 April, General Edward P. King, commander of the US and Filipino forces on the Peninsula, reached the inevitable conclusion that he had no alternative but to surrender. By that time all chance of halting the Japanese advance, much less launching a successful counterattack, had evaporated. Weak from hunger and disease and with many men badly wounded, the defenders on Bataan finally succumbed on 9 April 1942.

Between 60,000 and 80,000 American and Filipino officers and men were taken prisoner, far more than the Japanese could easily handle. There were also some 40,000 civilians who had been trapped on the peninsula. Somehow, the Japanese had to move the prisoners out of the way so that they could launch their assault on the final handful of US positions. As it was impossible to find transport for such large numbers of people to be moved to the nearest railhead, the only choice was for them to walk – almost seventy miles – in what is today referred to as the Bataan Death March.

Though resistance on the Bataan Peninsula had ended, US and Filipino troops still hung on in the handful of island fortresses which defended Manila Bay. Central to this defiant last stand were the guns and garrison on Corregidor.

Below: General Masaharu Homma, commanding the Philippine Expeditionary Force, comes ashore for the first time on Philippine soil at Santiago on Lingayen Gulf, 24 December 1941. (USNHHC)

Right: Japanese troops on the move towards the Bataan Front, March 1942. (USNHHC)

Below: Another view of Japanese troops during the advance on the Bataan Front in March 1942. As the fighting on the Peninsula ground towards its final conclusion, General Homma sent a message to General Jonathan M. Wainwright, the senior field commander of Filipino and US forces in the Philippines under General MacArthur. Copies of this communication were dropped over Bataan in beer cans. In this Homma praised the valiant stand made by the Americans and Filipinos but declared that he now had large enough forces and supplies 'either to attack and put to rout your forces or to wait for the inevitable starvation of your troops'. He urged Wainwright to be sensible and follow 'the defenders of Hong Kong, Singapore and the Netherlands East Indies in the acceptance of an honorable defeat'. To do otherwise, he declared, would be disastrous. (USNHHC)

Opposite page top: Japanese troops moving up to the Bataan front in preparation for the attack on 3 April 1942 – an offensive that resulted in the final collapse of the US-Filipino forces in the area. It began with the opening of an artillery barrage at 10.00 hours. The guns continued to pour down death and destruction on the Allied defenders until 15.00 hours – marking what had been described as 'undoubtedly the most devastating barrage of the campaign, equal in intensity, many thought, to those of the First World War'. (USNHHC)

Opposite page bottom: Japanese troops guard American prisoners of war, following the US capitulation on the Bataan Peninsula, at the beginning of the Bataan Death March on 9 April 1942. Note the Japanese photographer in the right foreground.

The brutality that came to mark the Death March often began the moment that an individual was captured, as Lieutenant Kermit Lay recalled: 'They pulled us off into a rice paddy and began shaking us down. There [were] about a hundred of us so it took time to get to all of us. Everyone had pulled their pockets wrong side out and laid all their things out in front. They were taking jewellery and doing a lot of slapping ... After the shakedown, the Japs took an officer and two enlisted men behind a rice shack and shot them. The men who had been next to them said they had Japanese souvenirs and money.'[3]

The executions may well have been because possession of such souvenirs and currency perhaps suggested that these items had been taken from Japanese servicemen who had been killed. (NARA)

Right: American prisoners of war with their hands tied behind their backs on the first day of the Bataan Death March, 9 April 1942. They have been identified as, left to right, Private First Class Samuel Stenzler, Private First Class Frank Spear and Captain James M. Gallagher.

All three were bound for having been found in possession of Japanese money, photographs or similar items that their guards considered to be contraband. None of these three men survived captivity. Gallagher was killed later the same day that this image was taken; Stenzler died in Camp O'Donnell on 26 May 1942; whilst Spear was executed in a PoW camp in Japan on 9 July 1945. (United States Marine Corps)

Above: A group of American prisoners under guard during the Bataan Death March in April 1942. Note the guard in the centre with the fixed bayonet. Captain William Dyess, commander of the 21st Pursuit Squadron, survived the Death March, but later recalled the Japanese behaviour: 'Their ferocity grew as we marched ... They were no longer content with mauling stragglers or pricking them with bayonet points. The thrusts were intended to kill.' (United States Marine Corps)

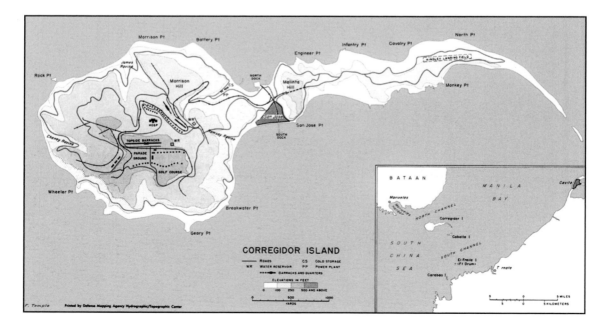

Chapter 1

THE ISLAND FORTRESS OF CORREGIDOR

Though the fall of Bataan ended all organized opposition on Luzon, it did not hand the Japanese the most valuable prize of all, Manila Bay. So long as Corregidor and its sister forts across the entrance to the bay remained in American hands, the use of the finest natural harbour in the Orient was, for the time being, denied them.

For centuries the island of Corregidor had guarded the approaches to Manila, initially as a lookout post to warn of the approach of hostile forces and then later as the first bulwark in the coastal defences of the Philippines' capital. After Spain ceded the Philippines to the United States in 1898, a major construction programme was taken in hand to further fortify Corregidor and supplement the existing defences of Manila Bay. By 1914, the work was complete, the powerful forts and batteries being designed to withstand attack from the heaviest battleships then afloat. The military post on Corregidor was named Fort Mills.

Below: A view of Malinta Hill from the waters of Manilla Bay. (NARA)

Corregidor, which is three-and-a-half miles long and one-and-a-half miles at its widest point, could boast twenty-three coastal batteries, mounting a total of fifty-six guns, including ten 12-inch mortars, eight 12-inch guns, two 10-inch and two 8-inch guns. The advent of aircraft in warfare saw the addition of anti-aircraft guns and searchlights during the 1920s. These weapons, though, were controlled by a fire control system that was obsolescent by 1941, but by that date they included the modern mobile 3-inch M3 guns which would, to some degree, prove effective against the enemy bombers in the fighting to come.

The defences of the three other islands in the entrance to Manila Bay were, proportionately, as formidable as those on Corregidor. Caballo, located just to the south of Corregidor, was the next largest in size. It housed Fort Hughes and by April 1942 had eleven batteries mounting a total of twenty guns of all types.

A further four miles south of Caballo was Fort Drum. This unusual fortress was constructed by turning the rocky outcrop of El Fraile Island into what appears very much like a concrete battleship. Drum had eight batteries with a total of thirteen guns.

Lastly, at the southern side of Manila Bay, just 500 yards from the shore, is the fortified island of Carabao. Better known as Fort Frank, it consisted of twenty-three guns mounted in eight batteries.

The most significant development on Corregidor during the inter-war years was the construction of a vast range of tunnels dug into the solid rock of the 390-foot-high Malinta Hill, where stores of all kinds could be housed safely from aerial bombardment. The main tunnel, constructed of reinforced concrete in 1932, was 1,400 feet long and thirty feet wide at its base, its walls forming an arch which curved twenty-feet above the floor. Along this main tunnel, twenty-five laterals branched out at either side, all of which were 150 feet long, except for one which led to a 300-bed hospital.

Covering the island were sixty-five miles of roads and trails, much of the heavy equipment on Corregidor being moved over an electric railroad, with more than thirteen miles of track leading to all of the important military installations. Electricity also drove the pumps of the twenty-one wells on the island, powered the cold-storage plants that kept perishable food refrigerated, maintained the ventilation in the underground tunnels, and operated the heavy coastal guns. The garrison's survival depended on the continued running of the electricity power plant and it was well protected from aerial bombardment.

Such were the main, but not the only defences of Corregidor. At some stage, if the enemy was to capture the island, they would have to land ground forces. So, to supplement the big guns and howitzers, barbed wire stretched along those beaches which offered possible landing sites, mines were laid and bunkers were erected deep in the ravines leading to the highest and main part of the island, Topside, where the bulk of the installations were to be found, as well as the intermediary Middleside. As might be guessed, the lowest part of Corregidor was called Bottomside.

Opposite page top: This aerial view of part of the area of Corregidor known as Topside is one of a series taken during a US government survey in the early 1980s. This area contained the headquarters, barracks, and officers' quarters, grouped around the traditional parade grounds. On the far left is the eastern end of Mile Long Barracks, in the centre foreground the ruins of the garrison cinema, to the right of that a barrack building with, beyond, the dome of the Pacific War Memorial Museum. (NARA)

Opposite page bottom: The southern area of Topside around Corregidor's lighthouse, looking north towards the distinctive remains of Mile Long Barracks. The concrete structures to the right of the light house are water tanks. (NARA)

Main image: Another aerial view of part of Topside looking east. The open area in the right foreground was the parade ground, while the white dome in the distance is the Pacific War Memorial Museum. Just in front of the museum, and slightly to the left, is the shell of the garrison cinema. The distinctive structure on the left is the ruins of the Mile Long Barracks. (NARA)

As the author Eric Morris once noted, 'for the Americans who lived and worked in the Philippines, that island archipelago was like India to the British, a hot and enervating land rich in servants and other amenities of colonial life.

Pampered and closeted from the grimy realities of the industrial world, the rigidly stratified society had over the years spawned an imperial aristocracy with a life-style that few of their countrymen at home would have recognized. It was a land where living was opulent yet cheap so that fortunes hard earned need not be squandered in support of "standards." Even those in more

Below: A view of the dock area on Corregidor taken looking out across Manila Bay towards the Bataan Peninsula. Corregidor is almost two islands, for at the junction of the 'head' and the 'tail' it narrows to just 600 yards and is barely above sea level. Unsurprisingly, this low area was referred to as Bottomside. In 1942 it contained two docks, the community of San José, shops, warehouses, a power plant, and cold-storage units. (USNHHC)

humble occupations among the white community could afford servants and the best the island had to offer.'[4]

The number of personnel on the island by late 1941 was around 13,000, of whom a little less than 2,000 were civilians. Whilst this sounds a strong force, only 4,400 or so were US Army soldiers with 1,352 Marines. The remainder were either US Navy personnel (1,715) or Filipinos, few of whom had ever received any proper infantry training. Two battalions of the 4th Marine Regiment under Colonel Samuel L. Howard were detailed to defend the beaches.

Below: The remnants of the South, or Navy, Dock in Bottomside, with, adjacent to it, the area of San José. It was from this dock that MacArthur famously departed Corregidor in March 1942. West of the narrow neck which connected the 'tail' with the 'head of the tadpole' was a small plateau that is called Middleside. A hospital, quarters for commissioned and non-commissioned officers, a service club, and two schools for the children of the island were all established in this area. (NARA)

Above: The area of North Dock which, also known as Army Dock, is located on the opposite side of Bottomside from South Dock. (NARA)

Opposite page: Directly to the east of Bottomside was Malinta Hill with its labyrinth of tunnels. In this view taken looking east, the western entrance of Malinta Tunnel can be seen roughly in the centre of the image. In the foreground is part of the island that is referred to as Bottomside, which is in effect the neck that connects the 'tail' and 'head' of the island. (NARA)

Below: The eastern entrance of Malinta Tunnel. Consisting of a main east-west passage 1,400 feet long and thirty feet wide, the Malinta Tunnel complex had twenty-five laterals, each about 400 feet long, that branched out at regular intervals from each side of the main passage. An underground hospital was established in its own group of tunnels to the north of the main passage. Opposite the hospital, under the south side of Malinta Hill, was the US Navy's tunnel system. (NARA)

Opposite page: An aerial view looking west along Corregidor at part of the island's 'tail'. A grass strip runway with hardened touchdown points at each end, Kindley Field, can be seen in the foreground. A US Navy radio intercept station was located on the 'tail' in 1942. (NARA)

Above: The final eastern portion of Corregidor pictured looking west towards Topside. East Point is just out of view to the bottom left. Corregidor's firepower was built around twenty-three batteries which, between them, mounted a total of fifty-six coastal guns, howitzers and mortars of various calibres. (NARA)

Opposite page top: Surrounded by the dense undergrowth that today covers much of Topside, this surviving artillery piece, a 12-inch M1898 gun, may well be part of Battery Smith. (NARA)

Opposite page bottom: The 12-inch M1895 gun of Battery Hearn, mounted on an M1917 long-range carriage, pictured from the air in the early 1980s. The two 12-inch guns of batteries Smith and Hearn provided the longest-range weapons on Corregidor in 1942. (NARA)

Overleaf: An aerial view of Battery Grubbs as it appeared in the early 1980s. The battery comprised a pair of 10-inch M1895 guns mounted on disappearing carriages. Unmanned at the start of the Second World War, it was not until early 1942 that the No.2 gun was made serviceable. The remaining gun had never been commissioned. The so-called Case Report, penned after the war, notes that 'on 11 April [1942] two bombs hit the emplacements damaging the power plant and No.1 tool room and bending overhead ammunition tracks. The battery was shelled daily from 12-16 April from Bataan. On 16 April No.2 gun was knocked out of action by a direct hit on the recoil cylinder … [and] the battery was abandoned.' (NARA)

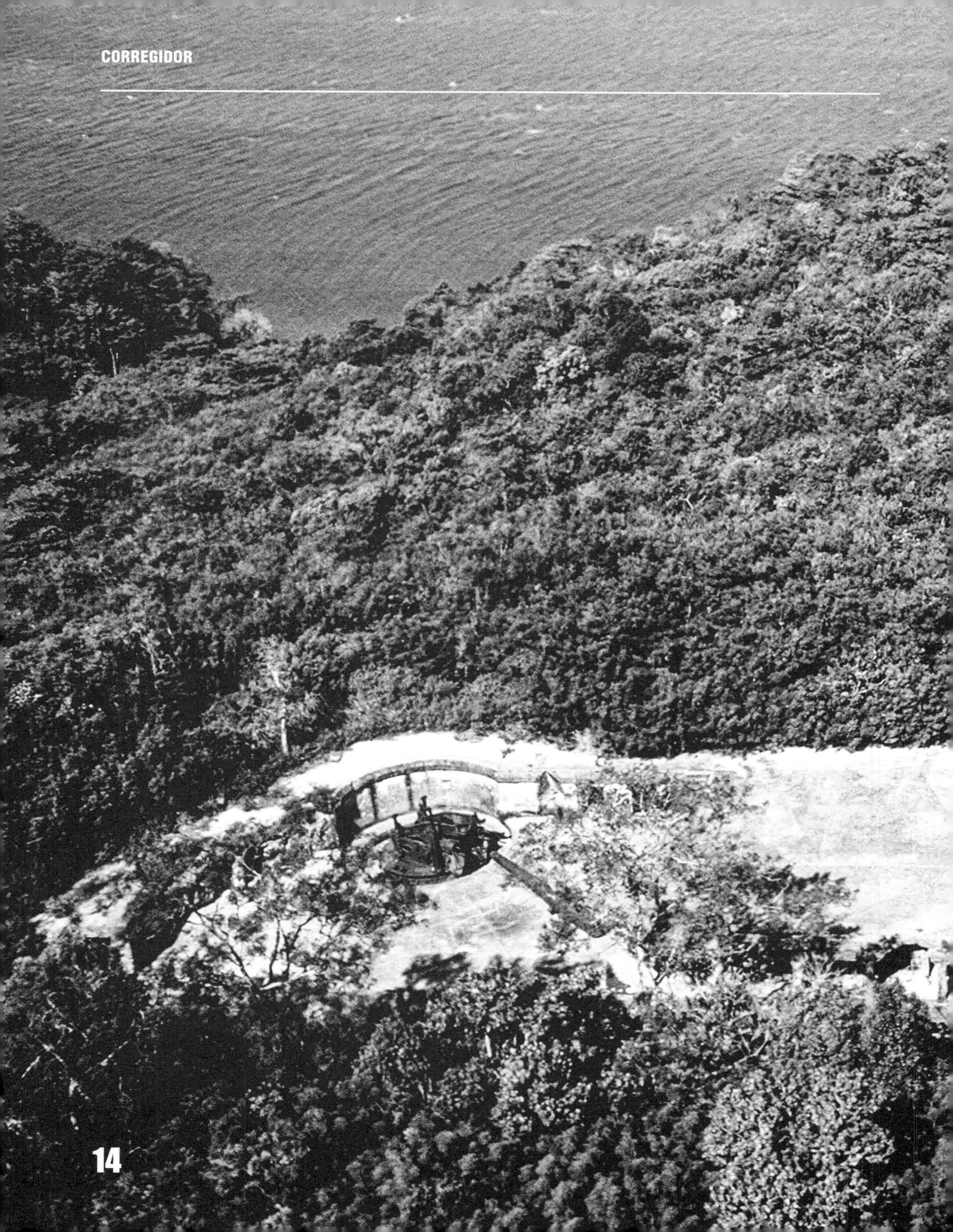

Above: The remains of Battery Cheney, which is located on the western part of Topside. Battery Cheney was equipped with two 12-inch M1895 guns mounted on disappearing carriages. At the time of the Japanese attacks, this position was manned by the 59th Coast Artillery. (NARA)

Chapter 2

UNDER FIRE

8 December 1941 – 8 April 1942

Despite the fighting on the nearby Bataan Peninsula, it was not until 29 December 1941, that the Japanese finally turned their full attention to Corregidor. At 11.54 hours that day, eighteen enemy bombers appeared over the island and targeted the various headquarters buildings and barracks.

Above: On **26 December 1941**, General MacArthur, Philippine President Manuel L. Quezon, and Francis B. Sayre, the US High Commissioner to the Philippines, and their staffs were moved to the relative safety of Corregidor. This picture shows the cars used by the General and his party after they were 'abandoned at Mariveles' prior to the group's 'escape' to the island fortress. (Australian War Memorial; P02305.050)

Escorted by nineteen fighters, the bombers approached Corregidor at an altitude of 15,000 feet and in regular V formation. The flight broke into smaller formations, of nine and three aircraft, which passed lengthwise over the island, then back, dropping 225lb and 550lb bombs on the headquarters buildings and barracks.

First Lieutenant Sidney F. Jenkins, with the 4th Marines, remembered the 'bombs screaming to earth with shattering explosions, the crack of AA guns, the neat "plop plop" of the AA shells

Above: An aerial view of the island of Corregidor taken in 1964. In the foreground is the main part of the island which, known as Topside, pointed towards the west. The island's 'tail' can be seen stretching eastward, with the result that this 'tadpole-shaped island' separated the Manila Bay entrance into a north and south channel. The southern tip of the Bataan Peninsula is out of view to the left.

It was at Topside that MacArthur was given accommodation when he arrived on the island. It was there, however, that he almost became a casualty himself on **29 December 1941**, as this communiqué issued at the end of the month revealed: 'General MacArthur narrowly escaped serious injury in a recent bombing raid in Bataan Province when a large bomb exploded less than ten feet away from him … During the raid the orderlies protected the General to the best of their ability providing him with a steel helmet and shielding him with their bodies. A piece of rock struck the General in the shoulder and one faithful orderly was wounded in the hand.'

This incident occurred during the first bombing on 29 December, at which point MacArthur had been in the garden of his cottage. Sergeant Domingo Adversario was the orderly who was wounded. The house was so badly damaged that MacArthur was moved to new accommodation in Bottomside, about one mile east of Malinta Tunnel.[9] (USMC Archives)

bursting all over the sky … There we were, the whole regiment flat on our bellies on the lower deck of Middleside Barracks.'

The attack lasted for thirty minutes, during which time almost fifty bombs were dropped – and there were more to come. Half an hour later, Japanese aircraft returned to continue the aerial bombardment. In the two hours of the attack, the Japanese unloaded approximately sixty tons of bombs on the island.

Above: In the face of growing shortages of food and ammunition, General MacArthur requested that US submarines be used to break the tightening Japanese blockade of Manila Bay. Though some senior naval officers disagreed, believing that the submarines should all be retained for offensive action against the enemy's advance, a number of relief missions were agreed to, if only as a morale-boosting gesture.

The first of these missions was undertaken by USS *Seawolf* (SS-197) which, commanded by Lieutenant-Commander Frederick Warder, is seen here later in the war. As the author Dr Edward C. Whitman noted, 'carrying only eight torpedoes in the tubes, *Seawolf* left Darwin on 16 January, bearing nearly 700 boxes of 50-caliber machine-gun bullets and 72 3-inch anti-aircraft shells. After threading through the Malay Barrier, the submarine headed north through the Molucca Passage and the Celebes and Sulu Seas toward Manila Bay, 1,800 nautical miles distant.'[10]

USS *Seawolf* arrived at Corregidor on **27 January 1942**. After being guided in through the defensive minefields by a PT boat, Warder off-loaded his cargo of ammunition. For the return trip, he took onboard sixteen torpedoes, a quantity of submarine spare parts, and twenty-five passengers identified for evacuation, equally divided between Navy and Army personnel. (NARA)

Above: US Marines on Corregidor celebrate the arrival of a fresh supply of cigarettes in early 1942. These men belong to the 4th Marine Regiment, which was augmented by Marines from Marine Barracks Olongapo and the formerly Cavite-based 1st Special Defense Battalion. Following the loss or scuttling of their vessels, many Asiatic Fleet sailors fought in the regiment's ranks as its 4th Provisional Battalion, eventually defending the beaches of Corregidor against repeated Japanese amphibious landing attempts. (NARA)

Fortunately, the main defensive structures had escaped relatively unscathed, but the barracks and the headquarters building, amongst many others, were badly damaged. Around 60 per cent of all the wooden structures were destroyed. Many of the other buildings were made of corrugated iron which, when hit, exploded into large metal splinters. According to Major Achille Tisdelle, after the raid Bottomside appeared to be 'one huge mass of jagged and bent sheet iron'.[5] As a result, headquarters was moved down into the Malinta tunnel.

The Japanese had not got away scot-free, however, with the anti-aircraft gunners bringing down thirteen heavy bombers and four dive bombers.

At this stage the other forts in Manilla Bay, those of Fort Drum on the islet of El Fraile, Fort Hughes on Caballo Island, and Fort Frank on Carabao Island, as well Bataan Peninsula itself, were still in US hands and their fire contributed to the success of the day. Command of all the forts in Manila Bay was in the hands of Major General George F. Moore.

The Japanese returned intermittently throughout the course of the following few days, but it was not until 2 January that they came back in force. Their approach concealed by cloud, fifty-four bombers broke through to deliver their deadly payloads. By the time they had departed, scarcely any part of Corregidor had escaped unscathed, and the island's railway line was smashed. The next four days saw the island pounded mercilessly until, on 6 January, Homma lost the major part of his air support, which was diverted for a pending attack on Thailand.[6] In addition, Homma's attention was focussed on Bataan and his assault on the US-Filipino positions the very next day.

With the enemy concentrating on seizing control of Bataan, Corregidor was temporarily ignored by the Japanese, but it was not forgotten. A Japanese artillery unit, called the Kondo Detachment after its commander, was spotted by observers on the mainland secretly erecting gun positions near Ternate, between six and eight miles from the island forts in Manila Bay. Initially, Major Toshinori Kondo's battery consisted of four 105mm guns and two l50mm cannon.

At 08.00 hours on 5 February, the Kondo Detachment opened fire, its principal target being Fort Drum, the so-called 'Concrete Battleship'. This tiny, but incredibly strongly defended island, was struck almost 100 times in a bombardment lasting three hours. The Americans tried to strike back, but the batteries on Corregidor had been designed to meet a seaborne attack and only a few guns could be traversed to counter the enemy. Both Fort Drum and Fort Frank were bombarded every morning for the following ten days, though Corregidor suffered only the occasional strike during this period.

The intensity of the bombardment increased, however, from the middle of February when Kondo's battery was reinforced by the addition of two 150mm howitzers. As it was clear that Corregidor could not hold out much longer, MacArthur, as mentioned previously, was ordered to leave the island. On 12 March command was delegated to General Jonathan Wainwright.

The pressure on Corregidor and the other forts was stepped up even further on 15 March after the Kondo Detachment was dissolved and a new much-larger unit, the Hayakawa Detachment, was formed under Colonel Masayoshi Hayakawa. The new detachment was composed of the 1st Heavy Artillery Regiment and the 2nd Independent Heavy Artillery Battery, both equipped with huge 240mm howitzers, which began to hammer the Manila Bay forts. Hayakawa opened fire on the morning of the 15th, with Fort Drum and Fort Frank receiving the heaviest treatment, the latter being hit by approximately 500 shells.

Day after day, the forts were subject to terrible punishment. Most of Fort Frank's armament was put out of action, and on one occasion a howitzer shell penetrated the eighteen-inch thick roof of one of its tunnels and exploded amongst a line of men, killing twenty-eight and wounding a further forty-six.

As well as the shells, bombs continued to rain down on Corregidor. A particularly intense period of aerial assault commenced on 24 January 1942. 'At 0924 the air raid alarm, the seventy-seventh of the campaign, sounded on Corregidor,' noted Louis Morton. 'One minute later, the first enemy flight of nine Army bombers came over the island to drop their 550- and 1,100- bombs. They were followed by the remaining Army squadrons which, in turn, gave way to the Navy's planes.

'The attack continued during the day and that night, when three more planes made a nuisance raid against the island. Altogether, forty-five of the sixty twin-engine bombers of the 60th and 62d Heavy Bombardment Regiments and the two squadrons of naval land-based bombers participated in the first day's attack [of this new offensive] to drop a total of seventy-one tons of bombs.

'The next day the Japanese sent only three Army squadrons, twenty-seven planes, against Corregidor; the Navy, a similar number. This pattern continued until the 29th, the Navy planes alternating with the Army bombers. In addition, small groups of planes came in over Corregidor every two or three hours "to carry out the psychological warfare and destroy the strong points, without failure".[7]

'The routine bombings continued steadily until 1 April, with at least one Army squadron attacking during the day and another at night. The Navy planes, which had no missions on Bataan, continued their bombardment of the island fortress in undiminished strength.'

For the men on Corregidor, it seemed as though they were living "in the center of a bull's-eye".[8] Worse, though, was to come.

Opposite page: Three officers of Corregidor's garrison inspecting defence positions during a respite from Japanese attacks. Left to right they are Lieutenant Colonel John P. Adams USMC, Colonel Samuel L. Howard USMC, and Major General George F. Moore. (USNHHC)

Below: A US Marine Corps Sergeant on Corregidor explains the use of the Lewis machine-gun to a group of Filipino soldiers. (NARA)

Right: The second US submarine to reach Corregidor was USS *Trout* (SS-202), which arrived on **3 February 1942**. Commanded by Lieutenant Commander Frank Wesley Fenno Jr., *Trout* had sailed direct from Pearl Harbor, on its second war patrol, on 16 January.

Arriving off Corregidor on the evening of 3 February, the submarine rendezvoused with *PT-34*, which then guided it through the minefield to the South Dock. There, *Trout's* much-needed cargo of 3,500 rounds of 3-inch anti-aircraft ammunition was unloaded. With the task complete, a number of spare torpedoes were then taken onboard.

At this point, the submarine was still too light to be trimmed adequately, so Fenno duly requested that a quantity of ballast be loaded aboard. What was carried down into the submarine, however, was not the expected sandbags or blocks of concrete, but two tons of gold bars and eighteen tons of silver pesos (the exact make-up of this precious cargo various from account to account).

These valuables had come from the vaults of twelve banks in Manila, the contents of which had been evacuated to Corregidor in the face of the Japanese onslaught – the paper currency had been burned to prevent it falling into enemy hands. As well as the gold and silver, *Trout* also took on board securities, mail, and US Department of State dispatches before submerging shortly before daybreak on the 4th. She then settled on the bottom in Manila Bay until the return of darkness.

That evening, *Trout*, having returned to South Dock, was loaded with further mail, securities and other valuables before she was escorted to open water. Fenno then set a course for the East China Sea, which the submarine reached on 10 February. When she arrived at Pearl Harbor on 3 March, the submarine transferred her valuable ballast to a cruiser, USS *Detroit*. This picture shows *Trout* coming alongside the cruiser. (USNHHC)

Above: US Marines seize a moment to relax during the Japanese bombardment and attacks on Corregidor. (NARA)

Opposite page: The unloading of the valuable cargo carried by USS *Trout* from Corregidor begins at Pearl Harbor, 3 March 1942. (USNHHC)

Right: Part of the unusual ballast carried by USS *Trout* on its return from Corregidor. *Trout* received eleven battle stars for its wartime service as well as a Presidential Unit Citation for her second, third, and fifth patrols. (USNHHC)

Opposite page: USS *Seadragon* (SS-194), pictured here from almost directly ahead, reached Corregidor on **4 February 1942**, the day after USS *Trout*. Operating out of Surabaja and having arrived off Luzon Point on the evening of the 4th, *Seadragon* then moved into Manila Bay, finally mooring at Corregidor at 22.03 hours. In the darkness, but under enemy artillery fire, working parties immediately set about unloading *Seadragon*'s cargo of thirty-four tons of rations and almost 12,000 gallons of petroleum, before taking on board two tons of spare parts, 1½ tons of radio and cryptographic equipment, including a vital *Purple* decoding machine, and twenty-three torpedoes.

The work was completed by 03.00 hours on the 5th, at which point *Seadragon* moved out to deeper water and rested on the bottom. She resurfaced after dark and embarked twenty-five passengers. At 19.46 hours, *Seadragon* got underway for the return journey to the Netherlands East Indies.

Among the evacuees who had boarded *Seadragon* at Corregidor were seventeen individuals considered vital to the Allied war effort, as Dr Edward C. Whitman explains: 'Before the war, one of the Navy's three principal cryptologic facilities, code-named *Cast*, had been located at the Cavite Naval Station and provided with a *Purple* machine capable of deciphering the Japanese diplomatic code. Then in mid-1940, the Navy transferred the facility to a newly-constructed tunnel complex on the eastern end of Corregidor. Because of the danger of compromising this extraordinary intelligence source should the cryptologic unit be captured by the enemy, the US high command placed top priority on evacuating *Cast* personnel from the Philippines when the loss of the islands became inevitable.'[11] (US Navy)

Below: The 12-inch gun at Battery Hearn as it appears today. It could fire a 1,000lb shell 30,000 yards every fifty-five seconds and had a full 360 degrees field of fire, though this was restricted by the surrounding terrain. It was served by thirty-three men under the command of Captain Samuel McReynolds of 59 Coast Artillery. On **12 February 1941**, Hearn began firing almost daily upon the Japanese guns of the Kondo Detachment. (John Grehan)

Above: Having navigated its way through the protective minefield, another American submarine, USS *Swordfish* under Lieutenant Commander Chet Smith, reached Corregidor on **19 February 1942**, at which point the crew promptly commenced loading a cargo of spare torpedoes.

The next day, Smith was ordered at short notice to embark a party of VIP passengers which included President Manuel L. Quezon, his family, Vice President Sergid Osmeña, Chief Justice Santos, and three senior officers from the Philippine Army. *Swordfish* evacuated the party to Panay, the sixth-largest and fourth most-populous island in the Philippines, where they boarded a motor tender.

This picture of *Swordfish* was taken a few months after the fall of Corregidor, whilst the submarine was off the coast of California. (US Navy)

Opposite page: General Douglas A. MacArthur, left, and Francis B. Sayre, the American High Commissioner in the Philippines, are pictured during an informal discussion on Corregidor. Like MacArthur, Sayre was evacuated from the island fortress, eventually returning to the United States. He was one of the passengers embarked on the submarine USS *Swordfish* at the same time as President Manuel L. Quezon on **20 February 1942**. (National Museum of the US Navy)

Above: General Douglas MacArthur (centre) with his Chief of Staff, Major General Richard Sutherland, in the Headquarters tunnel on Corregidor, **1 March 1942**.

On 27 January 1942, Secretary of State Cordell Hull suggested to Roosevelt that he should press MacArthur to make plans to evacuate from Corregidor. Indeed, on 2 February the Army's Chief of Staff, George C. Marshall, suggested that MacArthur's wife and son and one 'other person' (presumably MacArthur himself) should be added to an evacuation group.[12] By 22 February the US President had made up his mind.

The message ordering MacArthur's removal from 'The Rock' began to arrive in the communication centre in Malinta Tunnel at 11.23 hours the following day, 23 February. Having been decoded, it was handed to MacArthur at 12.30 hours. According to at least one of his biographers, Frazier Hunt,[13] MacArthur was far from impressed at the instruction, and initially refused to comply, drafting a terse refusal. The latter, though, was never sent and, having had time to consider his response in the cold light of day, was torn up by MacArthur. It would be a number of days before he actually departed from Corregidor. (NARA)

Opposite page: General MacArthur and his wife, Jean, pictured 'in a mess tent on the fortress island' of Corregidor in early March 1942. On the evening of 9 March, MacArthur summoned Wainwright and informed of the news of his departure, and that the hour to do so was imminent.

Sitting on the porch of his cottage, MacArthur provided the following explanation to Wainwright: 'Jonathan, I want you to understand my position very plainly. I am leaving for Australia pursuant to repeated orders of the President. Things have reached such a point that I must comply with these orders or get out of the Army. I want you to make it known throughout all elements of your command that I'm leaving over my repeated protests.'[14] (Historic Military Press)

Opposite page: Instead of waiting for the submarine that the US Navy had placed at his disposal, and which could not reach Corregidor until 13 to 15 March, MacArthur elected to travel to Mindanao by PT boat (short for Patrol Torpedo Boat). He duly announced to some of his staff that, 'We go with the fall of the moon; we go during the Ides of March'.[15]

As darkness settled down over Manila Bay on the evening of **12 March 1942**, MacArthur finally made his move. Along with his wife and son, Arthur, and a nurse for the child, MacArthur selected several members of his staff to accompany him. They included his chief and deputy chief of staff, the G-I and G-2, the senior signal, engineer, anti-aircraft artillery and air officers, a public relations officer, Sutherland's assistant, an aide, a medical officer, and a secretary.

MacArthur's immediate party embarked onboard *PT-41*, which was commanded by Lieutenant John D. Bulkeley; the other evacuees were allocated spaces on three other PT boats, *PT-32*, *PT-34* and *PT-34*.

MacArthur would later recall the moment: 'On the dock I could see the men staring at me. I had lost 25 pounds living on the same diet as the soldiers, and I must have looked gaunt and ghastly standing there in my old war-stained clothes – no bemedaled commander of inspiring presence. ... Through the shattered ruins, my eyes sought "Topside," where the deep roar of heavy guns still growled defiance, with their red blasts tearing the growing darkness asunder.'[16]

Two hours later, at 21.15 hours, the four small craft cleared the minefields and were soon speeding south. They set course for the northern coast of Mindanao, also commonly known as the Southern Philippines and the second-largest island in the Philippines.

Lieutenant Bulkeley is seen here while on the bridge of a PT boat during the spring of 1942. (NARA)

Right: Having sailed all through the night, the next morning Lieutenant Bulkeley's small flotilla put in at a tiny uninhabited island in the Cuyo group in the central Philippines. They finally reached the coast of Mindanao at daybreak on **14 March 1942**.

Already a celebrated PT-boat skipper, Lieutenant Bulkeley, who commanded Motor Torpedo Boat Squadron Three during the Philippines Campaign, was subsequently awarded the Medal of Honor. He is seen here being invested by President Franklin D. Roosevelt in July 1942. As we shall see in the following pages, Bulkeley, who had reached the rank of Rear Admiral and was serving as the President of the US Navy Board of Inspection and Survey, would return to Corregidor after the war. (USNHHC)

Above: Three days after MacArthur's departure from 'The Rock', a large party of forty-seven individuals, which included thirty-six cryptographers and linguists from the *Cast* intelligence station, as well as seven survivors from a US Navy PT boat which had broken down, were evacuated. The rescue vessel in this instance was yet another submarine, the Porpoise-class USS *Permit* (SS-178). It was *Permit* that had originally been allocated to MacArthur's own evacuation from 'The Rock'.

On its fourth war patrol *Permit* reached Corregidor on **15 March 1942**. By the time the embarkation of the passengers was complete, there were no less than 111 people crammed into the submarine. The night after leaving Manilla Bay, *Permit* encountered a small flotilla of Japanese destroyers, which the submarine promptly attacked, albeit unsuccessfully, with a pair of torpedoes. Predictably, the Japanese warships' response was swift: 'To escape the resulting depth-charge attacks, *Permit* was forced to stay down for 22 hours, putting a severe strain on the boat's oxygen supply, but on 7 April, [the captain] brought the boat and his grateful passengers safely into Fremantle, where he was then roundly criticized for agreeing to take so many personnel onboard.'[17]

This view of USS *Permit* was taken when the submarine was subsequently in port for a refit. (USNHHC)

Below: MacArthur and his party were subsequently flown to Australia in Boeing B-17s. In preparation for this stage of the journey, three B-17s had been flown out from Australia, two of which safely reached Del Monte airfield on Mindanao by midnight on **16 March 1942**.

Wasting little time, the evacuees were soon airborne, the overloaded aircraft taking-off at around 01.30 hours on the 17th. The five-hour flight took them over the captured enemy islands of the Celebes, Timor, and the northern part of New Guinea. The intention had been for the B-17s to land at Darwin, but the area was under Japanese attack at the time so the bombers were diverted to Batchelor Field in the Northern Territory. They landed at 09.00 hours on the 17th. The General was welcomed by a guard of honour provided by a six-man detail lead by Lieutenant Julian from Battery 'A' of the 102nd Coastal Artillery (AA Separate) Battalion, a US unit that had only arrived in Australia a few days earlier.

Of his journey, soon after his arrival MacArthur declared to the US Chief of Staff that, 'This hazardous trip by a commanding general and key members of his staff through enemy controlled territory undoubtedly is unique in military annals. I wish to commend the courage and coolness of the officers and men ... who were engaged in this hazardous enterprise. It was due entirely to their invincible resolution and determination that the mission was successfully accomplished.' MacArthur subsequently awarded Silver Stars to the crews of the two B-17s.

The memorial seen here was erected on the site of Del Monte airfield. It commemorates MacArthur's departure from the Philippines from this location.

Opposite page: During his onward journey from Darwin, MacArthur's train stopped at the rural railway station at Terowie, in South Australia, on **20 March 1942**. Greeted by a cheering crowd and expectant members of the press, MacArthur alighted to speak to them: 'The President of the United States ordered me to break through the Japanese lines and proceed from Corregidor to Australia for the purpose, as I understand it, of organising an American offensive against Japan, the primary purpose of which is the relief of the Philippines. I came through and I shall return.'

The following morning the *Advertiser* printed the interview with MacArthur under the headline: 'I Shall Return'. MacArthur seized on this theatrical phrase and used it repeatedly until his return to Manila in February 1945. This monument and plaque, on the platform at Terowie, marks that event. (Courtesy of 'Peterdownunder')

Above: General Douglas MacArthur, almost obscured by a sea of waving arms and hands, is greeted by a huge crowd following his arrival at the Menzies Hotel in Melbourne, Australia, on **25 March 1942**. A few days earlier, a US War Department communiqué reported that General MacArthur had arrived in Australia by air. He was accompanied by Mrs MacArthur and his son, his Chief of Staff, Major-General Richard K. Sutherland, and other senior air force and staff officers. (Courtesy of the Australian War Memorial; 043140)

Main Image: The submarine USS *Searaven* (SS-196) was no stranger to the waters of Manila Bay. During her first two war patrols in December 1941 and the spring of 1942, she ran supplies to the besieged American and Filipino troops on the Bataan Peninsula and Corregidor Island. Her third war patrol was intended to follow the same pattern.

It was on **2 April 1942**, that *Searaven* left Fremantle bound for Corregidor. Packed into her cargo spaces were 1,500 rounds of 3-inch anti-aircraft ammunition. However, desperately needed as they

were, these shells never reached their destination as *Searaven* was diverted whilst en route. The remainder of the patrol was undertaken in the vicinity of Timor Island of the Netherlands East Indies. On 18 April, she rescued thirty-two Royal Australian Air Force men from enemy-held Timor. Disaster struck five days later when a fire broke out in the submarine's main power cubicle, leaving *Searaven* completely stranded. Her sister submarine USS *Snapper* (SS-185), which was returning from a successful resupply run to Corregidor, came to her assistance and towed her into Fremantle.

Chapter 3

SIEGE

9 April – 4 May 1942

On 9 April, the US and Filipino troops on Bataan surrendered. The Japanese could now bring all their artillery to bear on Corregidor. Some indication of what the men experienced during the Japanese bombardment was described by Captain John Gulick, commander of Battery C, 91st Coast Artillery: 'To my terror it [the barrage] began to move toward us. There was a high rocky hill to my right and another to my left. Neither afforded any shelter whatsoever. We began to run, hoping to get around the side of the hill. The barrage walked after us at about a pace equal to our own.

'We rounded the hill and saw in front of us the ruins of the Ordnance warehouses blown up by bombs in December. The ground was heap after heap of concrete chunks and exploded 75 shells and casings. Suddenly the barrage behind us lifted and came down about 400 yds in front of us slightly to our left. We ran to the right. The curtain of fire lifted again and came down on our right moving towards us. Terror and desperation seized us. We were panting, sweating, and scared. It seemed as if the Jap artillery was playing cat and mouse with us …

'We ran down the old trolley tracks with barrages or concentrations behind and on both sides of us. Suddenly again up ahead shells began to land … We reached a drainage ditch and threw ourselves in it. Dead leaves had cloaked its depth so that we sank down about 3 feet. It was hot, dirty, and almost smothering. But we were so exhausted by terror and by running that we could only lie there panting and perspiring.'[18]

A similar disaster to that which occurred at Fort Frank was also to befall Fort Mills when, on 29 April, a day marked by particularly heavy shelling, two Japanese 240mm shells fell on a group of men standing by the west portal of Malinta Tunnel. Fourteen were killed and seventy were wounded. Nurse Lieutenant Juanita Redmond was on duty in the hospital lateral: 'We worked all that night, and I wish I could forget those endless, harrowing hours. Hours of giving injections, anesthetizing, ripping off clothes, stitching gaping wounds, of amputations, sterilising instruments, bandaging, settling the treated patients in their beds, covering the wounded that we cannot save.'[19]

With the Japanese devoting all their attention to Fort Mills and the bay forts, the intensity of the bombardment both from the air and the ground was staggering, as more enemy guns found firing positions at points on the Bataan Peninsula. In time, at least thirty-seven batteries were able to bring their weapons to bear on the battered, beleaguered island of Corregidor.

During that latter half of April and the first few days of May, the Japanese mounted more than 300 air raids and delivered hundreds of thousands of shells on Corregidor. Eventually, most of the island's big guns were wrecked, with just one 12-inch mortar and a mobile 155mm gun able to attempt counter-battery fire.

Opposite page: Newspapers in the US announce the fall of Bataan on **9 April 1942**, a moment that heralded the start of the Japanese siege of Corregidor. (NARA)

EXTRA

Oakland Tribune HOME EDITION

36,000 U.S. MEN FEARED LOST IN FALL OF BATAAN

| Corruption In Defense | ...HUR, WAR CABINET PREPARE COUNTER-DRIVE | Two British Cruisers Sunk | AGREEMENT REPORTED | Retreat to Corregidor |

JAPS TRAP 36,800 AS BATAAN FALLS

HOME EDITION THE POST and ENQUIRER

Extra

2 Ally Cruisers, 1 Axis Ship Sunk

NIPPON PLANES INDIA OCEAN OWN BRITISH

Base in Ceylon Bombed

Stimson Tells Heroic **Efforts to Send Help**

Gasoline

BATAAN COLLAPSES!
Japs Crush American Defenders

San Francisco AMERICA FIRST *Examiner* **6 AM EXTRA**

IN THE NEWS	New Orders Issued To Rush Dock Work	CEYLON NAVAL BASE BOMBED BY JAPANESE	Foe Overcomes Exhausted Forces in Philippines
	Unions Back Longshore Program		
	War Styles For Women Stay Smart	Axis Raid in Libya; Suez Push Seen	U.S. Chief of Staff Meets Churchill

Whilst considered to be the second most bombed place during the war after the Island of Malta, it is estimated by one renowned historian that Corregidor was 'battered and blasted by more tons of high explosive than any other spot of its size on the planet'[20]. No final tally exists of the number of bombs and artillery rounds that struck the island, but, according to Bill Sloan, early on the morning of 2 May, at the start of a typical combined enemy air-artillery bombardment, two of Wainwright's staff officers began counting the number of explosions.

They determined that on average at least a dozen bombs and shells hit the island every minute for five straight hours – a total of 3,600 rounds, delivering an estimated 1.8 million pounds of explosives. After that, they stopped counting.

Yet still the garrison refused to give in. It was clear to General Homma that Wainwright and his men might not be bombed into submission. He was left with no choice but to consider mounting an amphibious operation to capture the island that had defied him for months.

Left: The last supplies to reach the besieged fortress of Corregidor arrived soon after the surrender on Bataan on **9 April 1942**. As mentioned previously, they were delivered by the submarine USS *Snapper*. Loaded with some forty-six tons of food and 29,000 gallons of diesel oil, *Snapper* had earlier sailed from Mactan Island. On reaching Manila Bay, the stores were transferred to the submarine rescue vessel USS *Pigeon* (ASR-6). Having then embarked twenty-seven evacuees, *Snapper* weaved her way back through the Japanese blockade before setting course for Fremantle, evading Japanese destroyer patrols on the way.

This view of *Snapper* was taken later in the war whilst the submarine was docked at the Mare Island Navy Yard in California. (USNHHC)

Above: The precious cargo that USS *Pigeon*, seen here, had loaded from *Snapper*, right under the enemy guns overlooking the south channel off Corregidor, was hastily transferred to the shore. In the days that followed, *Pigeon's* crew spent the daylight hours ashore and returned to their ship for night operations. The latter included dumping Philippine coinage in the south channel. *Pigeon* continued to serve until the afternoon of 4 May 1942, when a bomb from a dive bomber exploded on her starboard quarter. She sank in eight minutes. Thankfully, her crew was on land at the time. (NARA)

Opposite page: On **9 April 1942**, the first Japanese artillery, a 75mm battery, reached the area of Cabcaben, a community on the very southern tip of the Bataan Peninsula. Lying directly across the water from Corregidor, in plain sight of the defenders its guns promptly opened fire. It was, remarked Colonel Paul D. Bunker, commander of the Seaward Defenses on Corregidor, 'a crucial point in our operations – a milestone'.

This Japanese propaganda image is of artillery bombarding Corregidor during the siege in April and May 1942. (USNHHC)

Opposite page top: While moored at the eastern point of Corregidor, USS *Finch* (AM-9), seen here before the war, was damaged by the near miss of a Japanese bomb on **9 April 1942**. The explosion tore her seams open, whilst fragments of the bomb pierced the hull. The entire crew landed safely, and *Finch* was abandoned. She foundered the next day, 10 April 1942. (USNHHC)

Opposite page bottom: At the same time as the Siege of Corregidor began following the fall of Bataan, the venerable submarine tender USS *Canopus* (AS-9), already damaged during early Japanese attacks on 29 December 1941 and 1 January 1942, was ordered to be sunk in order to deny her use to the enemy. On **10 April 1942**, under her own steam she was duly backed off from the dock into deep water and scuttled. This picture of *Canopus* was taken in Shanghai prior to the outbreak of war. (USNHHC)

Below: Pillars of smoke rising from Corregidor during the Japanese bombardments of April and May 1942. By **12 April 1942**, many of the Japanese batteries were in position and at 06.00 hours that day it could be said that the bombardment of Corregidor began in earnest. Most of the fire came from 75mm and 105mm guns; it would be a few days before the majority of the 150mm guns joined the barrage. It was also on the 12th that the batteries on Cavite opened fire on Corregidor, while Japanese aircraft made nine separate attacks against the island. (USNHHC)

Left: As the Japanese guns continued to pound Corregidor, the tempo of the onslaught increased steadily. The first American positions to be put out of action were the seacoast guns on the north shore facing Bataan and visible to the Japanese. By **14 April 1942**, three 155mm batteries, each with two guns, and one 3-inch battery of four guns had been disabled. The vulnerable directors and height finders on Topside were badly damaged, although the operators succeeded in keeping at least one in operation at all times. Another casualty in the Siege was the 12-inch gun at Battery Hearn, which was forced to cease fire as it was an easy target from the high ground in Bataan. As this picture shows, the extent of the damage inflicted upon it can still be seen. (John Grehan)

Below: As the days passed, the Japanese intensified the pressure on Corregidor and the frequency of the artillery and aerial attacks grew during the latter part of April. On **18 April 1942**, for example, a number of 240mm howitzers, which had been moved from Cavite, added their weight to the bombardment. This large crater is still visible at Battery Hearn on Corregidor. (John Grehan)

Above: The shelling never really stopped. With over 100 pieces ranging in size from 75mm guns to huge 240mm howitzers, the Japanese were able to maintain fire almost without a break. Taken on **24 April 1942**, this picture shows men sheltering in Lateral No.12 off the Malinta Tunnel. Code machines and telegraph operators of the Signal Corps message centre are behind the partition at the right rear. The photograph was taken from the island on 3 May 1942, by the last submarine to call there. (USNHHC)

Opposite page top: A view of surviving 12-inch mortars at Battery Way, one of the most important gun emplacements on Corregidor. Battery Way consisted of four 12-inch mortars which, being obsolete, had been out of service for a number of years before the Japanese attack. Three of the four mortars were re-activated and, operated by personnel from Battery E of the 60th Coast Artillery, recently evacuated from Bataan, returned to service on **28 April 1942**, when they retaliated against enemy positions on Bataan. (Shutterstock)

Opposite page bottom: It is said that some of the most effective American counter-battery fire was delivered by batteries Geary and Way, both equipped with 12-inch mortars. However, being relatively exposed, no sooner had Battery Way gone into operation then it was targeted by Japanese guns and aircraft. This recent picture shows battle damage to the wall around Battery Way. (John Grehan)

Above: Further damage to Battery Way caused by the Japanese attacks. By the time the Japanese landings began on 5 May 1942, only one of the mortars was still serviceable, the other two having been damaged beyond repair. (John Grehan)

Right: Between 9 April and the end of the month there were 108 air raid alerts on the Manila Bay forts, amounting to some eighty hours. The vast majority of the attacks were directed against Corregidor. This 'aerial blitz' came to a head on **29 April 1942**, Emperor Hirohito's 41st birthday. The day began with an air alarm, the 260th of the campaign, at 07.30 hours, when two flights of bombers came over Fort Hughes and three dive bombers hit the South Dock on Corregidor and the Malinta Tunnel entrances. Here Japanese Army Mitsubishi Ki-21 *Sally* bombers are pictured during a sortie over Corregidor. (USNHHC)

Above: Created for the modern-day visitor, this is a representation of one of the Malinta Tunnel laterals being used as an office. For a time the Malinta Tunnel became not just the headquarters of the United States Army Forces in the Far East, but also the seat of the Philippines government. (John Grehan)

Opposite page: Japanese bomber units were not the only ones to celebrate Emperor Hirohito's birthday on **29 April 1942**. Between them, that day the various enemy artillery batteries launched a particularly vicious bombardment that saw some 10,000 shells be fired at Corregidor. Here Japanese guns can be seen bombarding Corregidor at night during April or May 1942. (USNHHC)

Main Image: Even as the Japanese noose tightened around Corregidor, efforts were still being made to resupply the garrison. On 27 March 1942, the submarine USS *Spearfish* (SS-190) began its third war patrol, sailing from Fremantle in Australia. The patrol took the submarine to the Sulu Sea and the Lingayen Gulf off the Philippines. On 17 April, she despatched an enemy cargo ship of approximately 4,000 tons, and, on the 25th, she sank *Toba Maru*, a 6,995-ton freighter.

On the night of **3 May 1942**, *Spearfish* slipped into Manila Bay, where, unable to reach the docks at Corregidor itself, she rendezvoused with a small boat carrying twenty-seven evacuees, of whom twelve were nurses, from Corregidor. The last people to escape from the island, they were transported to Fremantle, which *Spearfish* reached on 20 May.

Spearfish was the last US warship to sail from Manila Bay before the final Japanese victory in the Philippines. This picture shows *Spearfish* underway on the surface, possibly off Mare Island Navy Yard, after its rescue mission to Corregidor. (USNHHC)

Above: A group of 'US nurses who had escaped from Corregidor' pictured in Australia sometime in June 1942. It is likely that some, or even all, of these women were part of the group rescued by USS *Spearfish*. In all, eight American submarines successfully ran the Japanese blockade of Corregidor, the last being *Spearfish*, before the beleaguered fortress surrendered. (Australian War Memorial; 012386)

Opposite page: One of the passengers embarked on USS *Spearfish* on **3 May 1942**, was Lieutenant, Junior Grade Ann A. Bernatitus, a US Navy Nurse Corps officer – pictured here later in the war. Having served throughout the Japanese attack on the Philippines, Bernatitus would later recall being evacuated to Corregidor:

'On the 8th [April], we were transferred to Corregidor. That's when the front lines collapsed. I don't remember what kind of boat it was, probably one of the things that used to ply between Corregidor and Canacao. Anyway, it was after supper. We ate at 4 o'clock. About 8 o'clock they told us to take what we had – and we didn't have much. …

'Finally, when the boat arrived, we got on. It must have been a ferry. I remember sitting in the passageway on a wicker chair. I was carrying my camera; I never gave that up and brought it home with me. They were shooting back and forth over us. When we got to Corregidor, I don't think the people there knew we were coming because that night we had to sleep two in a bunk … I was less scared on Bataan than I was on Corregidor. When the Japanese bombed, the whole place just shook.'[21]
(National Museum of the US Navy)

Below: A view of part of the hospital wards in Malinta Tunnel on Corregidor, in which nurses such as Lieutenant Bernatitus worked, as they appeared in 1942. Despite such facilities, as the Siege reached its climax at the end of April, the first signs of malnutrition began to make an appearance among the garrison. It was about this time that cases of Beriberi and scurvy began to be noticed. (US Armed Forces Institute of Pathology)

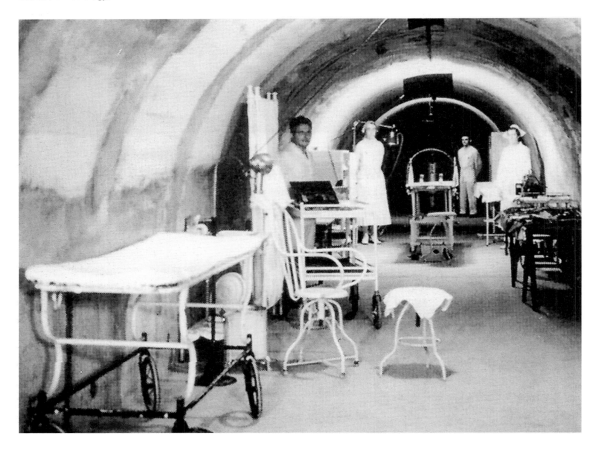

Opposite page: After nearly a month on Corregidor, Lieutenant Bernatitus remembers being selected to be one of the passengers to embark on USS *Spearfish* on **3 May 1942**. 'They told us we would meet after dark in front of Wainwright's headquarters,' she later recalled. 'But then the Japanese started shelling us, so they canceled [*sic*] us. We were told to meet I think 2 or 3 hours later. Your name was called, and you stepped out of the crowd because everybody was gathered around to see this. Wainwright shook your hand and wished you Godspeed and he said, "Tell them how it is out here."

'And then I got in a car and they took us out of the tunnel down to the dock. Everything was pitch-black, just some trees standing with no leaves, no nothing, charred. When we got down there, we got on a boat that was even smaller than the one that took us to Corregidor. Then we shoved off.

'We had to go through our own mine fields to get to the submarine. We learned later that it was taking us so long to get out there that the submarine wasn't sure Corregidor hadn't already fallen.

'Finally, we saw this dark shape and we came alongside of it. You could hear the slapping of the

water between the two objects. Then someone said, "Get your foot over the rail". And then someone just pulled me, and then the first thing I knew I was going down the hatch. I got down there awfully fast. On May 3rd we were evacuated from Corregidor. There were six Army officers, six Navy officers, eleven Army nurses, and one Navy nurse. There was also one civilian woman, and two stowaways – one Navy electrician's mate and one who was with the Army transport.' *Spearfish* arrived in Fremantle seventeen days later.

For her actions at Bataan and on Corregidor, in October 1942 Bernatitus became the first American recipient of the newly instituted Legion of Merit. At the same time, Albert Murray, a renowned painter of numerous admirals and dignitaries, completed a portrait of her at the Corcoran Gallery in Washington – this being the oil painting seen here. At the time, Bernatitus was stationed at National Naval Medical Center in Bethesda, Maryland, and on a number of occasions she took the trolley or bus from Bethesda to the Corcoran to sit for Murray. (USNHHC)

Opposite page: One of the US ships sunk during the Japanese bombardment of Corregidor was the tug *Trabajador*, almost certainly a victim of shelling from enemy artillery positions on Bataan. Completed by the Hong Kong-Whampoa Dock Co. in 1931, she operated with the Visayan Stevedoring Co. into 1941, following when she was pressed into service with the US Navy. *Trabajador* remained on the bottom of Manila Bay until after the end of the war. She was subsequently raised, when this image was taken, repaired, and renamed *Resolute*, remaining in service as a tug, in the Philippines, into the late 1970s. (USNHHC)

Above: The minesweeper USS *Tanager* (AM-5), seen here during a pre-war exercise, withdrew to Corregidor on or about Christmas Day 1941.

On board were the equipment and staff of the Commandant, 16th Naval District, Rear Admiral Francis W. Rockwell. As the US Navy's History and Heritage Command points out, *Tanager* 'subsequently operated out of Corregidor on inshore patrol duties. In ensuing months, *Tanager* and her dwindling number of sister ships and former China river gunboats lived a furtive, hunted existence. *Tanager* served almost until the bitter end. On **4 May 1942**, the day of the commencement of the Battle of the Coral Sea, the minesweeper was hit by shore battery fire from Japanese guns emplaced on Bataan. Mortally hit, she sank off Corregidor that day.' (National Museum of the US Navy)

Left: As the Siege dragged on conditions in the tunnels on Corregidor worsened. 'Dust, dirt, great black flies, and vermin were everywhere,' wrote Louis Morton, 'and over everything hung the odor of the hospital and men's bodies. During an air attack, when the large blowers were shut off, the air, offensive at best, became foul and the heat almost unbearable. Sometimes the lights failed and the gloom of the tunnel flickered into darkness … Crowded into enforced intimacy, on short rations, and under constant strain, men grew tense and irritable.'[22] This is the west entrance to the Malinta Tunnel as it appears today. (John Grehan)

Overleaf: The main east to west passage in the Malinta Tunnel is 1,400 feet long and thirty feet wide. Completed in 1932, it had twenty-five laterals branching out from it at regular intervals along both sides, as well as a separate underground hospital with its laterals.

Maude R. Williams, a hospital assistant, was one of the many who sought shelter in the tunnels during the Siege: 'Under the deepening shadow of death, life on Corregidor took on a faster, more intense tempo. The smallest and most simple pleasures became sought after and treasured as they became increasingly rare and dangerous – an uninterrupted cigarette, a cold shower, a stolen biscuit, a good night's sleep in the open air. There was a heightened feeling that life was to be lived from day to day, without illusions of an ultimate victory.'[23]

At the beginning of May, Japanese artillery and aircraft opened their final phase of the Siege by unleashing a bombardment which in Homma's own words would 'overwhelmingly crush' Corregidor's defences and 'exterminate' its defenders.

Even General Wainwright reached the conclusion that Corregidor's fate had been sealed. 'It took no mental giant,' he wrote, 'to figure out, by May 5, 1942, that the enemy was ready to come against Corregidor'. (Shutterstock)

Chapter 4

THE JAPANESE LANDINGS

5-6 May 1942

Homma hoped to take Corregidor with 'a sudden blow' in which his infantry and tanks would mount two separate amphibious assaults on successive nights at opposite ends of the island. Such a plan was forced upon Homma as he lacked sufficient craft to land all the troops in one go. It was expected that Fort Mills would fall on Day 2 of the operation, which would begin on the evening of 6 May, the landing craft departing shortly after dark to deposit the troops on the island at 23.00 hours.

Below: A number of small Japanese boats carrying elements of the landing parties underway off Corregidor Island at the time of its capture in May 1942. Despite all of their intensive planning and preparation, the Japanese landings suffered problems from the very beginning. Having miscalculated the tides around Corregidor, the initial waves of invaders were pushed off course and instead of going ashore at the intended landing beaches between Infantry Point and Cavalry Point, they landed 1,000 yards to the east, near North Point. (National Museum of the US Navy)

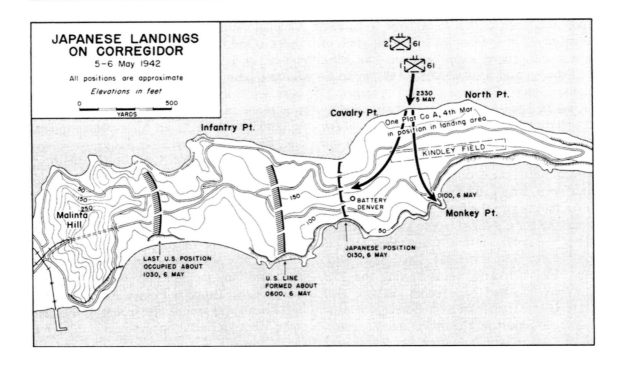

JAPANESE LANDINGS
ON CORREGIDOR
5-6 May 1942

All positions are approximate

Elevations in feet

0   500
YARDS

North Pt.

Cavalry Pt.

2330
5 MAY

One Plat Co A, 4th Mar
in position in landing area

KINDLEY FIELD

Infantry Pt.

150

0100, 6 MAY

BATTERY
DENVER

Monkey Pt.

50

100

50
150
250

Malinta
Hill

LAST U.S. POSITION
OCCUPIED ABOUT
1030, 6 MAY

U.S. LINE
FORMED ABOUT
0600, 6 MAY

JAPANESE POSITION
0130, 6 MAY

In preparation for the attack, the Japanese, as we have already seen, stepped up their bombardment of Corregidor even further. First Lieutenant Jenkins, whose Reserve Company of the 4th Marines was guarding Corregidor's East Sector, remembered how it was 'practically impossible to get any rest or to repair any damage to our positions and barbed wire. Our field telephone system was knocked out; our water supply was ruined (drinking water had to be hauled from the other end of the island in large powder cans) … Corregidor was enveloped in a cloud of smoke, dust, and the continuous roar of bursting shells and bombs. There were many more casualties than we had suffered in the previous five months.'[24]

On 5 May 1942, President Roosevelt had the following message transmitted to General Wainwright: 'During recent weeks we have been following with growing admiration the day-by-day accounts of your heroic stand against the mounting intensity of bombardment by enemy planes and heavy siege guns. In spite of all the handicaps of complete isolation, lack of food and ammunition, you have given the world a shining example of patriotic fortitude and self-sacrifice.

'The American people ask no finer example of tenacity, resourcefulness, and steadfast courage. The calm determination of your personal leadership in a desperate situation sets a standard of duty for our soldiers throughout the world. In every camp and on every naval vessel soldiers, sailors, and marines are inspired by the gallant struggle of their comrades in the Philippines.'

By the afternoon of 5 May 1942, General Wainwright knew the Japanese amphibious assault was looming. Agents in Manila had informed him that the enemy's 4th Division had concluded its landing exercises and that thousands of bamboo ladders, which presumably would be used to scale the cliffs of Corregidor, had been delivered to Homma's units. With a full moon forecast for the night of 5/6 May, Wainwright could well have assumed that his counterpart would make his next move in a matter of hours, not days.

Above: Japanese troops step ashore on Corregidor. This is a print of a captured Japanese photograph that was copied in 1942. The initial landing of 790 Japanese troops on **5 May 1942** quickly bogged down due to surprisingly fierce resistance from the American and Filipino defenders, whose 37mm artillery exacted a heavy toll on the invasion fleet. It was a bloodbath.

Observers at Cabcaben described the scene as 'a spectacle that confounded the imagination, surpassing in grim horror anything we had ever seen before'.[25] Another observer recalled that the 'Beach defense officers at the scene reported that the slaughter of the Japanese in their barges was sickening'. (National Museum of the US Navy)

As it turned out, the Japanese were indeed about to play out their final act in their capture of the Philippines. On 5 May, forces led by Major General Kureo Taniguchi, the commander of the 4th Division's infantry group, began embarking on the landing craft and barges that would transport them across Manila Bay. Later that evening an intense bout of shelling descended on the beaches between North Point and Cavalry Point.

At about 21.00 hours, sound locators detected the distinctive throbbing of engines as a large flotilla of craft approached Corregidor from the eastern side of the Bataan Peninsula. Barely an hour passed before the first wave of Homma's invasion force was spotted closing in on Corregidor's 'tail'. The command post in Malinta Tunnel immediately instructed all defence troops to their posts. At 22.30 hours, the order went out to 'prepare for probable landing attack'.

The full moon was just rising when, shortly before midnight, the Japanese artillery fire suddenly ceased and 'its bass roar was replaced by the treble chattering of many small arms'. A few minutes later a runner arrived at the command post with the news that the Japanese had landed at North Point.

Above: Around midnight on **5 May 1942**, a second wave of Japanese troops hit the landing beaches. They too suffered at the hands of the defiant defenders. Such was the scale of the enemy losses, that the total number of casualties for both landings are estimated at several hundred; one Japanese officer claimed that only 800 men of the 2,000 allocated to the invasion reached the shore and got off the beaches. This captured Japanese photograph is captioned as showing enemy troops deploying a flamethrower against the defenders on Corregidor during the invasion. (NARA)

Opposite page: Despite their losses, some of Homma's men, chiefly of the 1st Battalion, 61st Infantry, had managed to fight their way ashore near North Point at about 23.10 hours on 5 May 1942. After a sharp, but fierce engagement with elements of Company A, 4th Marines, who were dug-in along the north shore from Malinta Hill towards the eastern tip of the island, these Japanese troops were able to establish a beachhead on Corregidor. This picture shows some of these soldiers moving inland later on **6 May 1942**. (USNHHC)

Above: Taking advantage of the confused situation in the early hours of 6 May, the Japanese pushed out from their beachhead. In doing so, by 01.30 hours they had established a north-south line across the island between Infantry Point and Cavalry Point. It was also about this time that the invaders started landing their own artillery and tanks.

One US Marine, in his post on Denver Hill – in the area where the Japanese line was located – heard voices that were 'not American'. It was then that he realised he was on the front-line. 'The place,' he recalled, 'seemed to have Japs all over it'.[26] Here, also pictured on **6 May 1942**, Japanese troops and tanks continue their advance across Corregidor. (USNHHC)

Opposite page: Throughout the early hours of **6 May 1942**, the American defenders launched a number of counterattacks, often involving men who were ill-equipped or ill-trained for such a task. That said, one such assault, launched soon after 06.00 hours, took the enemy by surprise. What was described by one Japanese officer as an 'obstinate and bold counterattack' pushed the invaders back, allowing the Americans to make some welcome gains.

At his headquarters on Bataan, Homma, on hearing of these counterattacks was growing increasingly concerned at the progress of the battle.

By this point he was already becoming mindful of his losses, dwindling supplies of ammunition and the difficulties he faced in getting reinforcements ashore thanks to a lack of suitable landing craft. According to his own recollections, at one point he declared, 'My God, I have failed miserably on the assault'.

As it transpired, Homma's fears were misplaced. His men were repeatedly breaking through the American lines.

Then, just before 10.00 hours, three tanks that the invaders had managed to get ashore on Corregidor finally went into action. At this point the fighting swung irretrievably in the Japanese commander's favour. 'The effect of the tanks,' recalled Colonel Yoshida, 'was more than had been anticipated'. In this picture, Japanese troops can be seen crossing a field or parade ground near an accommodation block on Corregidor as they begin to consolidate their victory on the 6th. (USNHHC)

Below: There was, in reality, little that the Americans and Filipinos could do to stop the Japanese when they landed on 5 May. By 10.00 hours the next morning, **6 May 1942**, the situation for the Americans was critical. 'The troops on the front line were pinned down securely,' wrote Louis Morton. 'Attempts to move forward were discouraged by the enemy's heavy machine guns and light artillery; movement to the rear only brought the men under fire from the heavier guns on Bataan and strafing aircraft. The tanks were in action and there were no weapons with which to stop them.'[27]

When Japanese troops reached positions only a matter of yards from the entrance to Malinta Tunnel, where around 1,000 wounded soldiers were seeking shelter, Wainwright took the only decision open to him. In the words of one commentator, he opted 'to sacrifice one day of freedom in exchange for several thousand lives'.

Orders were duly issued for the Japanese to be informed of the surrender. Consequently, at 10.30 hours, General Lewis Beebe, Wainwright's Chief of Staff, stepped up to the microphone of the 'Voice of Freedom', the radio station that broadcast from Corregidor. In a tired but clear tone he read a message addressed to General Homma 'or the present commander in chief of the Imperial Japanese Forces on Luzon'. That message was from General Wainwright and it contained his offer to surrender.

Here, Japanese troops celebrate on and around one of the artillery pieces, possibly at Battery Hearn. (USNHHC)

Opposite page: In his final communication from Corregidor, Wainwright informed President Roosevelt that, 'There is a limit of human endurance, and that point has long been passed'. Instructions were issued that all weapons over .45 calibre were to be destroyed by midday on **6 May 1942**. At that time, the American flag on Corregidor would be lowered and burned and a white flag hoisted. It was at 12.30 hours when Homma learnt that a flag of surrender was flying over the island.

For those sheltering in the Malinta Tunnel complex, many of whom were 'dirty, hungry, and completely exhausted', one of the last acts taken was to open the quartermaster lateral, allowing those present to take whatever he or she wanted. It was an opportunity for a last meal before the Japanese moved in. This picture captures the moment that an American flag is lowered on Corregidor after the island's capture. (USNHHC)

Below: In his messages transmitted from Corregidor on that fateful day, Wainwright included the following: 'With broken heart and head bowed in sadness but not in shame, I report … that today I must arrange terms for the surrender of the fortified islands of Manila Bay … Please say to the nation that my troops and I have accomplished all that is humanly possible and that we have upheld the best traditions of the United States and its Army … With profound regret and with continued pride in my gallant troops, I go to meet the Japanese commander.'

For a number of reasons, the two opposing commanders did not meet until 17.00 hours on **6 May 1942**, when Wainwright and his staff were taken to Homma's headquarters on the Bataan Peninsula. The meeting opened brusquely, all formalities or courtesies brushed aside, when Wainwright removed his formal signed surrender note from his pocket and handed it to Homma. After some discussion, during which Wainwright declined to surrender any other remaining pockets of US or Filipino resistance in the Philippines, Homma abruptly stood up, and, after issuing a series of curt instructions to the Americans, walked out of the meeting.

Wainwright and his party returned to Corregidor to consider their next step. In their absence, however, the Japanese had forged ahead with their assault and occupation plans, in many cases taking little notice of the white flags that had been raised. On 6 May, for example, eighty-eight tons of bombs were dropped by the Japanese, a good part of them after the surrender.[28]

As more enemy soldiers and equipment were landed, American troops were rounded up and the task of clearing out the many occupants of the Malinta tunnels started. This image shows a Japanese field gun on Malinta Hill, overlooking the island's eastern portion, as they tightened their grip in the hours following their invasion. (USNHHC)

Below: Late on **6 May 1942**, Wainwright, looking out over his former command in the darkness, could see the fires lit by the newly arrived Japanese troops burning across Corregidor. Accepting that there was no longer any point in delay, he asked to be taken, as Homma had instructed that afternoon, to the local Japanese commander. He was duly escorted around Malinta Hill to San José.

There, in the ruins of the market square, he came face-to-face with Colonel Gempachi Sato, the commander of the 61st Infantry. 'There was no discussion of terms,' noted Louis Morton. 'The surrender was unconditional, and the document drawn up by the two men contained all the provisions Homma had [earlier] insisted upon. Wainwright agreed to surrender all forces in the Philippines, including those in the Visayas and on Mindanao, within four days.' The signing of the document was completed at about midnight.

In this image, victorious Japanese soldiers pose for the photographer by a captured artillery piece on Corregidor, presumably on the 6th. (USNHHC)

Above: A Japanese photograph showing US soldiers and sailors surrendering in front a debris covered tunnel entrance at Corregidor on **6 May 1942**. (NARA)

Above: Some of the defenders of Corregidor being herded by Japanese soldiers out of the fortress tunnels where they had been besieged. (Australian War Memorial; P02018.103)

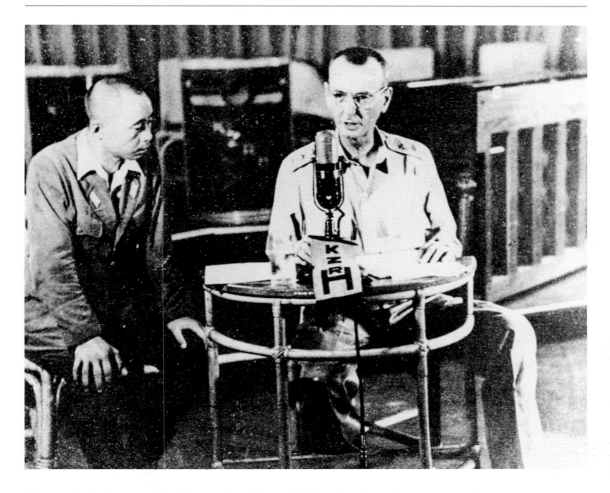

Above: Following the fall of Corregidor, General Wainwright broadcast a surrender message over the KZRH radio station on **7 May 1942**. The following excerpt formed part of Wainwright's speech: 'By the powers vested in me, I order General William Sharp, Commanding General of American-Filipino Forces on Mindanao and Visayans, to instruct his men to surrender. On the 6th, I met Lieutenant General Homma, the Japanese Commander, and discussed the terms of the surrender. He told me that he would not accept any proposals of surrender unless all troops under my command capitulate. In the interest of humanity, it is useless to continue to resist, so I have decided to surrender. All American and Filipino troops will throw down their weapons immediately.'

It was more than a month before this message had filtered through to all Allied forces in the Philippines and that, with the exception of a number of small detachments in extremely isolated areas, they all finally surrendered. As a result, it was not until 9 June 1942, that General Wainwright was notified that all organized resistance had ended. 'Your high command,' the Japanese then informed him, 'ceases and you are now a prisoner of war'. (USNHHC)

Opposite page: News of the Japanese capture of Corregidor is announced on the streets of Manila, **6 May 1942**. (USNHHC)

Main Image: Lieutenant General Masaharu Homma reviews the Japanese Army's victory parade which was held in Manila after the fall of Corregidor. Note the artillery towed by tracked vehicles. The original Japanese caption states: 'America's harsh claims in Greater-East-Asia were obliterated. The Filipinos

were released from the tyrannical hands of the Americans, and the policy of Asia for the Asiatics were instituted … The day of the fall of Corregidor marked the day of victory for the Japanese spirit over the culture and spirit of the Anglo-Americans.' (USNHHC)

Above: The Japanese flag is raised during the victory parade held in Manila after the fall of Corregidor in May 1942. Emperor Hirohito's forces had conquered the Philippines. (USNHHC)

Chapter 5

ESCAPE, CAPTIVITY AND OCCUPATION

1942-1944

On Thursday, 7 May 1942, the Japanese Imperial Headquarters announced that Emperor Hirohito's armed forces had 'at 8 o'clock today completely occupied Corregidor Island and other forts on other islands in Manila Bay after having succeeded in landing on Corregidor at 11:15pm on May 5th'.

Below: American and Filipino prisoners pictured in the immediate aftermath of their capture on Corregidor. On **7 May 1942**, MacArthur issued a statement in which he said: 'Corregidor needs no comment from me. It has sounded its own story at the mouth of its guns. It has scrolled its own epitaph on enemy tablets. But through the bloody haze of its last reverberating shot, I shall always seem to see a vision of grim, gaunt, ghastly men, still unafraid.' (NARA)

Corregidor's defeat in effect marked the fall of the Philippines and capped Japan's domination of Asia. It was a defeat through which Japan gained probably the best harbour in the Orient, excellent bases from which to stage and supply their garrisons to the south and east, as well as a large population to contribute to their planned Greater East Asia Co-Prosperity Sphere.

Victory it might have been, but Japan's timetable for the conquest of Australia and the rest of the Pacific had been severely disrupted. Homma had planned for the American defeat in the Philippines to have been achieved by the end of February, only to see it set back by many months.

It was a delay for which he paid the price. The campaign was hardly over when the Imperial General Headquarters relieved Homma of command and ordered his return to Tokyo.

Japanese losses in the Battle for Corregidor amounted to some 900 dead and 1,200 wounded. From the Allied side, the figures were slightly lower, being around 800 and 1,000 respectively. Whilst a few managed to slip through the net, or at least attempted to, the great majority of the island's garrison, roughly 11,000 US and Filipino personnel, men and women, were marched off to captivity.

For the next three years, the Japanese maintained their grip over Corregidor and its defences. It was only as the Allied advance crept closer to the Philippines that prospect of its liberation became an increasing reality.

Opposite page: The fate of those nurses left behind in the Philippines and on Corregidor became a cause célèbre in the United States, as this recruitment poster, redolent of similar events in the First World War, testifies. (NARA)

Below: A group of nurses photographed on Corregidor in the days after their capture when the island fell to the Japanese. (USNHHC)

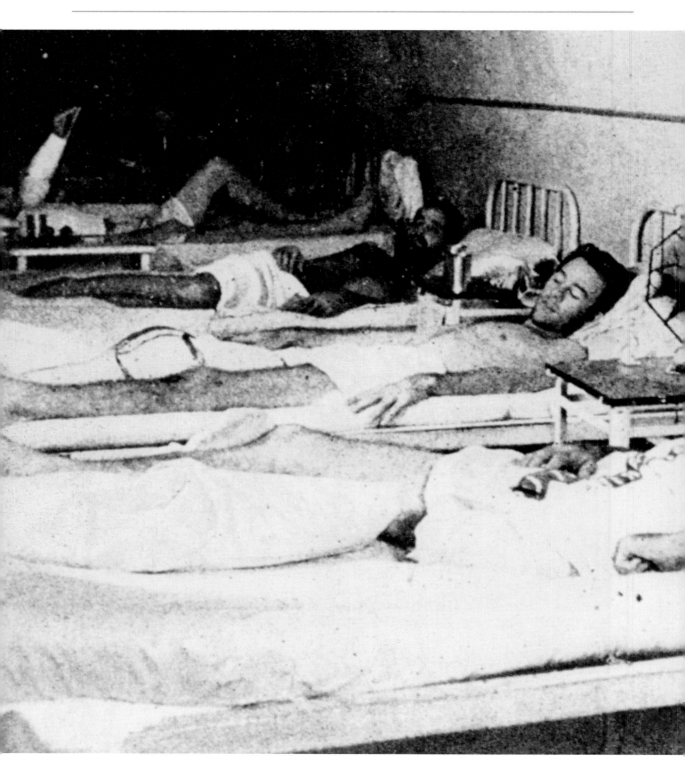

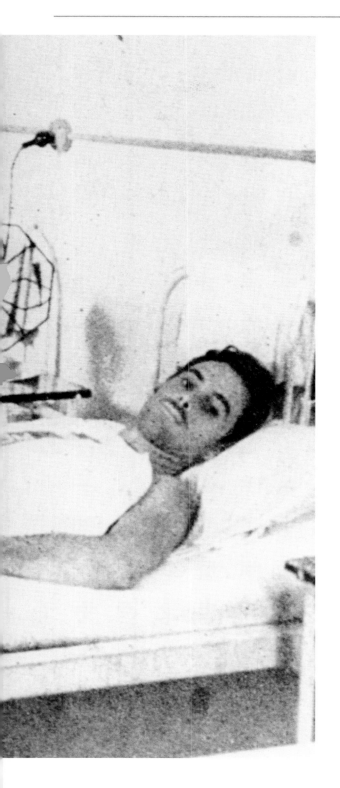

Opposite page: Injured American prisoners of war, photographed in one of Corregidor's hospital wards in the tunnels, after the island's capture.

On **8 May 1942**, President Manuel L. Quezon delivered a talk on the fall of Corregidor via a radio broadcast. He reiterated Field Marshal Douglas MacArthur's earlier promise to return to the Philippines (see Chapter 2) and help drive out the Imperial Japanese forces. (USNHHC)

Above: By the time Corregidor surrendered to the Japanese on 6 May, all US vessels in the area had been scuttled or destroyed (*Canopus, Luzon, Oahu, Quail, Genesee, Napa, PT-31, PT-32, PT-33, PT-35* and *PT-41*) or lost to enemy action (*Mindanao, Pigeon, Tanager, Finch, Bittern,* and *PT-34*). This is one of these vessels – the river gunboat USS *Oahu* (PG-46), which was sunk by enemy gunfire off Corregidor on 5 May 1942. Parts of the wreck are reported to still be visible near East Point. (National Museum of the US Navy)

Main Image: Having operated variously as a tug, a ferry, and a target tow in the Philippines, USS *Genesee* (AT-55), seen here in the First World War, was also lost off Corregidor on 5 May 1942, though in her case she was scuttled to avoid capture. (USNHHC)

Below: A light draft monitor, USS *Napa* (AT-32) was another ship scuttled on 5 May 1942, the order to do so being given at about 01.30 hours that day. The US Navy's History and Heritage Command takes up the story: 'Most of the crew, with provisions, personal belongings and small arms, were transported, via small boats, to Corregidor Island. *Napa* was then towed 500 yards out from the beach. The skeleton crew opened the magazine flood valves and made 3 openings through the hull in the fire and engine room. At 0500 *Napa* was abandoned. The CO, Ens. P.B. Wingo, and the remaining crew members proceeded to Corregidor. From that island they watched their ship remain afloat throughout the day and then, after nightfall, sink into the bay.

'The crew of *Napa* then joined the crews of other similarly fated ships. Taking up small arms, they were incorporated into the 4th Marine Regiment, in which they helped man the beach defenses.' This picture, believed to have been taken at Guam, shows USS *Napa*, with some of her crew, before the war. (USNHHC)

Opposite page: This view of the scene on the beach of Caballo Island near Corregidor, taken after its capture by the Japanese, is dominated by the wreck of the half-sunken ship in the background. It is believed that this is USS *Finch*, which, having been abandoned on 9 April 1942, foundered the next day. (USNHHC)

Main Image: Most US Navy personnel from the sunk or scuttled ships became Japanese prisoners of war. However, some were able to escape and join guerrilla groups.

For their part, the commanding officer of USS *Quail* (AM-15), Lieutenant Commander John H. Morrill II, and seventeen members of his crew reached Darwin on **6 June 1942**, after enduring a month at sea in their ship's motor launch. Damaged by enemy bombs and guns, *Quail*, which had been working to keep open a swept channel to Corregidor's South Harbor, was scuttled on 5 May 1942, to prevent her capture. This picture shows *Quail*'s motor launch and its occupants in Darwin harbour after their remarkable journey. (USNHHC)

Above: Lieutenant Commander John H. Morrill II photographed in Australia after his escape from Manila Bay in USS *Quail's* thirty-six-foot motor launch. The following account provides an insight into Morrill's journey:

'Some of the crewmembers were just too exhausted to even contemplate such a journey, but 17 men decided to join Morrill and take their chances with the sea rather than surrender to the Japanese. At 10:15 on the evening of 6 May 1942, Lieutenant Commander J.H. Morrill and 17 of *Quail's* crewmembers set off on a remarkable journey south towards Australia. They initially traveled at night and hugged the coastline as their 36-foot motor launch plodded along at three knots. The men camouflaged the tiny vessel with green fronds and branches and painted it black so that it would look like a harmless native fishing boat. They avoided numerous Japanese aircraft, destroyers, minesweepers, and patrol boats as they continued southwards along the Philippine coastline …

'By 13 May, they headed into the more open waters of the Sibuyan Sea and moved past the southwest end of Masbate Island in the central Philippines. They passed a Japanese tanker along the way, but the tanker ignored them, possibly thinking that they were either pirates or fishermen. They reached Cebu on May 15.'[29]

Travelling via Tandag on north-eastern Mindanao, which they reached on 17 May, and Fisang Island, north of Timor in the East Indies (24 May), the intrepid escapers eventually reached Melville Island, just north of Darwin, on 4 June. Having been given supplies of water and food, they set out on the last leg of their journey and slowly made their way into Darwin Harbour. Twenty-nine days after leaving Corregidor, they had reached safety after covering a staggering 2,060 miles – all with no sextant, no decent charts, and only a pocket watch as a chronometer. (USNHHC)

Below: The eighteen members of USS *Quail*'s crew pictured following their arrival at Darwin, Australia, in June 1942. Standing, from left to right, are: E. Watkins; L. Bercier; B. Richardson; R. Rankin; R. Newquist; J. Meeker; J. Stringer; C. Weinmann; and H. Haley. Kneeling, left to right, are: G. Swisher; R. Clarke; N.G. Cucinello; G. Head; J. Morrill; D. Taylor; J. Steele; P. Binkley; and E. Wolslegel.

Two weeks later, thirteen of the men were back in the Pacific, fighting the Japanese as part of the crews of US Navy destroyers. Morrill, Gunner Taylor, and the remaining three men were transferred to duty stations in the United States. Binkley was killed in action, and another crewman died before the war ended.

Fourteen of the crew retired with twenty or more years' service in the US Navy. Lieutenant Commander Morrill received the Navy Cross and was eventually promoted to the rank of Rear Admiral. (US Navy)

Opposite page: Machinist N.G. Cucinello, one of Lieutenant Commander John H. Morrill's intrepid group of evaders, is invested with the Silver Star by Secretary of the Navy, Frank Knox, during the commissioning ceremony of USS *Iowa* on 22 February 1943. Machinist Cucinello was awarded the Silver Star for his heroism in scuttling USS *Quail* during the fall of Corregidor. The citation for this award reads as follows:

'The President of the United States of America takes pleasure in presenting the Silver Star to Chief Watertender Nicholas George Cucinello, United States Navy, for gallantry in action against the enemy while serving on board the U.S.S. *Quail* (AM-15), after that vessel was ordered scuttled in the Philippine Islands on 6 May 1942.

'After it became apparent that the fall of Corregidor was imminent, Chief Watertender Cucinello volunteered with others to assist their commanding officer in performing this task, left the shelter of Fort Hughes and raced through exposed areas of the Fort Hughes dock while that place was under heavy artillery barrage. Upon their arrival at the dock they found their ship's small boat sunk and, accordingly, had to swim 200 yards to another boat anchored at the dock. While in the water Chief Watertender Cucinello and his comrades swam through Japanese artillery fire and numerous airplane strafing attacks, but reached the small boat nevertheless. He then proceeded with his comrades to the *Quail*, continuing to dodge artillery and airplane machine gun fire en route, until the minesweeper was reached and scuttled. By his great effort, Chief Watertender Cucinello materially assisted in accomplishing this difficult and dangerous task. His conduct throughout reflects great credit upon himself, and was in keeping with the highest traditions of the United States Naval Service.' (USNHHC)

Right: William F. Harris pictured during his graduation from the United States Naval Academy, Annapolis, Maryland in 1939. Harris served in Company A, 1st Battalion, 4th Marines and was captured by Japanese forces during the fall of Corregidor. He subsequently escaped from his PoW camp, only to be recaptured while trying to make his way to Guadalcanal in 1943. He was then held in Ōfuna PoW camp. Harris remained in the Marines after the war and was recalled to active duty during the Korean War. He was killed during the Battle of Chosin Reservoir in 1950. (USMC Archives)

Above: Named 'Soochow', the dog seen here had been adopted by the 4th Marines as their mascot during their time in China in the late 1930s. He accompanied his keepers into captivity following their surrender on Corregidor, subsequently enduring the same trials and tribulations as the Marines themselves. Once he was liberated, he was flown to California and became the mascot of Marine Corps Recruit Depot at San Diego. (USMC Archives)

Opposite page: A photograph of Corregidor taken from a gun emplacement on Caballo Island after its capture by the Japanese in May 1942. (USNHHC)

Above: Heavy shells on ready-service carts in Battery Crockett after Corregidor's capture by the Japanese, May 1942. (USNHHC)

Opposite page: American and Filipino prisoners of war working near the entrance to a tunnel on Corregidor under Japanese guard. (USNHHC)

Below: A wrecked mortar emplacement on Caballo Island after its capture by the Japanese in May 1942. (USNHHC)

Above: US Navy torpedoes photographed on Corregidor, after its capture, by the new Japanese occupiers. (USNHHC)

Below: Japanese tanks and troops on Corregidor after its capture. Note the former US Navy vehicle in foreground. (USNHHC)

Above: The ruins of Battery Crockett on Corregidor photographed after the Japanese conquest of the island in May 1942. (USNHHC)

Below: A dismounted and wrecked US Navy 1.1-inch anti-aircraft gun mount photographed on Corregidor after its capture by the Japanese in May 1942. (USNHHC)

Above: A wrecked coastal artillery gun on Corregidor, photographed after its conquest by the Japanese in May 1942. (USNHHC)

Above: One of the defence mortars on Corregidor, photographed following its capture by the Japanese in May 1942. (USNHHC)

Opposite page: On **12 May 1944**, Captain John M. McNicholas, attached to a 14th Air Force reconnaissance squadron, flew from an advanced airbase in China to undertake a sortie over Corregidor.

Taken by him, this picture is captioned as being the 'first photo made since the Japs took over in 1942'. (NARA)

Below: Also taken by Captain John M. McNicholas during his sortie on **12 May 1944**, this photograph, labelled as the 'first coverage of Philippines since 1942', has been annotated.

Location 1) is stated as simply 'Corregidor'; 2) Caballo Island; 3) Caballo Bay; 4) Kindley Field; 5) Seaplane base; 6) North Channel; and 7) Bataan. (NARA)

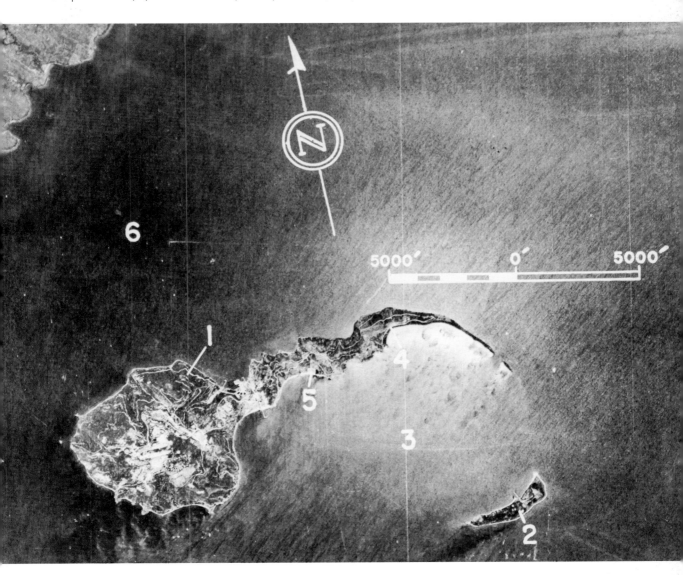

Above: The fall of Corregidor was never far from the mind of many Americans. Here President Roosevelt's second American War Plant Tour arrives at Camp Joseph T. Robinson, in Arkansas, on **18 April 1943**, the presidential procession pictured passing between two rows of troops presenting arms. Note how the vehicle nearest the camera is named *Corregidor*. (NARA)

Chapter 6

THE DAWN OF LIBERATION

1944-1945

Above: Corregidor was bombed for the first time by US aircraft on **24 January 1945**, two days after General MacArthur designated the island as a target (sources disagree on the date of the first strike, some giving it as the 22 or 23 January). Taken during that first attack, the caption to this image states:
   'Well-aimed bombs, exploding at the mouth of a huge underground storage cave, blew up a large ammunition dump. Cargo ships and wharves also were blasted. The entire target area was in flames when the "jungle air force" Liberators turned homeward. The Corregidor strike was another "first" for the 13th AAF, which made the opening daylight land-bombing strikes at Yap, Truk and Balikpapen, Borneo.' (NARA)

CORREGIDOR

The fall of Corregidor marked the low point in US operations in the Pacific but, even before its occupation by the Japanese, plans were being drawn up for its recapture and for MacArthur to fulfil his promise to return to the Philippines.

Slowly, but with increasing momentum, US forces struck back at the Japanese, wrecking their fleets and their aircraft at Midway, Truk, Leyte Gulf and in the Philippine Sea, and liberating the Solomons, the Gilbert and the Marshall Islands, Guam and the Marianas. By the fall of 1944, MacArthur's Sixth Army, supported by the U.S. Fifth Air Force and the U.S. 3rd and 7th fleets, was poised to retake the Philippines.

The first steps in the liberation of the Philippines were taken at Leyte on 20 October 1944. But for General MacArthur, the Philippines meant Manila. The Philippines' capital had been his home when his father had been the Governor-General. It was where he had lived with his first and second wives, and where his son had been born. After fighting his way, island by island, across the Pacific, he was poised to make good on his promise to liberate the Philippines – and to return home.

After the successful landings on Leyte, when he first stepped foot back on Philippine soil, General MacArthur's next move was to transport his forces closer to the main Philippine island of Luzon. The first step in this was the taking of the island of Mindoro, which was achieved in December 1944. From there, MacArthur intended to land on the beaches of the Lingayen Gulf, on the north-west of Luzon, before advancing upon Manila.

Right: Corregidor under attack by B-24 Liberators of the US 7th AAF. The original caption states that 'bombs from the first two elements send pillars of smoke hundreds of feet into the sky (center) while a stick of thousand pounders blast gun emplacements along the cliff tops (right)'. (NARA)

Leading the amphibious assault on 9 January 1945, were the 40th Division and the 37th Division of the US Sixth Army. Casualties were heavy, as the Japanese fought with their habitual determination, but the American troops secured a foothold and began to drive southwards towards Manila.

Three weeks later, on 31 January, the U.S. Eighth Army landed unopposed at Nasugbu in southern Luzon and began moving north toward Manila. Japanese forces gave ground, being squeezed into a pocket around the capital, where Rear Admiral Sanji Iwabuchi, commander of the Imperial Japanese Navy's 31st Naval Special Base Force, was determined to fight it out to the death with his 12,500 men despite being ordered to evacuate the city by the commander of the 14th Army, General Yamashita.

The Battle of Manila began on 4 February, with the 37th Infantry Division driving south through the city while the 1st Cavalry Division undertook an enveloping movement from the east. The battle for Manila raged on throughout February, the city burnt and blasted into rubble, its citizens murdered by the Japanese or killed by American shells. But by 1 March only one building, the Finance Ministry, remained in Japanese hands. It was reduced to rubble by the following day and when American troops wrestled control of its ruins, the bloody Battle of Manila was brought to an end.

The taking of Manila cost the U.S. more than 1,000 killed and 5,500 wounded; 16,665 Japanese were killed. It was, though, the Filipinos who suffered both the destruction of their city and also the heaviest casualties, with possibly as many as 240,000 losing their lives in one of the most dreadful episodes of the Second World War.

As part of the fighting to liberate the Philippines, on 16 February 1945, US troops, mirroring the events of some three years earlier when the Japanese had been on the ascendency, overcame the last organized enemy resistance on the Bataan Peninsula. Now, even as the fighting in Manila continued, operations to retake Corregidor Island could now begin in earnest.

But even at this stage, information concerning the isolated Japanese garrison on the island was so scanty that the estimate of 850 troops 'had, in fact, hardly attained the status of an educated guess, even though it was necessary to use that figure as a basis for planning'.[30]

The reality was that the Japanese had over 5,000 men on Corregidor, all but 500 of whom were naval personnel. As with all the other islands in Manila Bay, Corregidor was garrisoned by the Manila Bay Entrance Force, which was commanded by Captain Akira Itagaki IJN whose headquarters was on Corregidor.

Opposite page: On **13 February 1945**, Allied warships joined in the bombardment of Corregidor. The cruisers and destroyers of Task Group 77.3 initially directed most of their fire at the north side of the island where the Japanese defences were considered to be their strongest. Rear Admiral Russell S. Berkey's ships were unable to silence all the return Japanese fire from Corregidor and had made large inroads in their ammunition supply in the attempt. Therefore, Admiral Kinkaid despatched three heavy cruisers and five destroyers from Lingayen Gulf to augment the fire of the five light cruisers and nine destroyers Berkey already had under his command. The new arrivals joined in the bombardment at about 12.30 hours on 15 February.

This picture shows Rear Admiral Berkey speaking to another warship, the Royal Australian Navy's London-class cruiser HMAS *Shropshire*, via electric megaphone or loud hailer from the bridge of his flagship, USS *Phoenix* (CL-46), during the pre-landing bombardment of Corregidor on 15 February 1945. (USNHHC)

Reporting in turn to Admiral Iwabuchi in Manila, Itagaki's forces included three provisional infantry companies and two provisional artillery batteries from the Japanese Army, all of which had been assigned defensive sectors.[31]

Not anticipating an airborne attack, Itagaki had deployed his troops for defence against an

Above: The cruisers and destroyers of Task Group 77.3 directed most of their fire at the north side of Corregidor, where the Japanese defences appeared strongest. Here, Rear Admiral Russell S. Berkey is pictured directing operations on board USS *Boise* (CL-47) during the bombardment in February 1945. Note the anti-flash clothing worn by some of the men. (USNHHC)

amphibious assault. His most heavily defended positions were at James, Cheney, and Ramsay ravines, as well as Malinta Hill. Over half of his troops were ready for action at these points; the remainder of the garrison, as well as manning small defensive positions scattered across the island, was generally kept in reserve on Malinta Hill or in the tunnels below.

Above: Photographed from USS *Phoenix* a column of five light cruisers leaving Subic Bay en route to bombard Corregidor, **13 February 1945**.

   They are, from left to right, USS *Boise*, USS *Denver* (CL-58), USS *Cleveland* (CL-55), and USS *Montpelier* (CL-57). Note the signalman in the foreground. (USNHHC)

Opposite page: At the same time as the naval and aerial bombardment, minesweepers began clearing the waters around Corregidor. While assisting these operations on **14 February 1942**, the destroyer USS *Fletcher* (DD-445) was hit by an enemy shell. One of USS *Fletcher*'s crew was Watertender First Class Elmer Charles Bigelow. He fought the blaze that engulfed the destroyer, but in so doing he was badly injured. He succumbed to his wounds the next day. For his valour and personal sacrifice, Bigelow was posthumously awarded the Medal of Honor. This vignette, drawn by Mario DeMarco for *Navy Times*, outlines Bigelow's actions. (USNHHC)

Above: As well as hitting USS *Fletcher* on **14 February 1945**, the Japanese shore guns also damaged the motor minesweeper *YMS-48* and struck the destroyer USS *Hopewell* (DD-681) – the minesweeper was so severely mauled that it later had to be sunk. This picture of USS *Hopewell* was taken just after she had been hit by a shell off Corregidor. (USNHHC)

Above: A close-up of some of the damage to USS *Hopewell* by the shell fired by a Japanese shore battery. At the time, the destroyer had been laying smoke and manoeuvring to assist the stricken *YMS-48*. In the course of this, *Hopewell* was hit four times, which put her battery control station out of commission. There was a total of seventeen casualties. (USNHHC)

Opposite page: Bombs dropped by B-24 Liberators of the 494th Bombardment Group burst on Corregidor during a raid on **14 February 1945**. The island was attacked by the aircraft of this unit on 24, 25 and 26 January 1945, as well as 1, 2, 3, 6, 11, 12, 13, and 14 February. A history of the 494th Bomb Group states:

'Corregidor and Caballo were the targets for twelve major strikes by our B-24s from 24 January to 14 February, two days before the landing of ground forces on this sentinel of Manila Bay. A total of 267 sorties were flown, and over 665 tons of bombs were dropped. During these strikes many direct hits were placed on the American-named gun batteries, Crockett, Cheney, Wheeler, Grubbs, Morrison, and Ramsey. A number of buildings with their contents of war materiel suffered direct hits, as did water tanks, docks, jetties, a cargo vessel off the island, personnel areas, anti-aircraft positions, and fuel dumps. A tremendous explosion and fires were caused at Caballo.

'After each visit the tiny islands were left smoking and exploding as the hoarded stores of Japanese occupation were reduced to debris and ashes. Anti-aircraft fire, at first meager, inaccurate to accurate, dwindled to nothing under these attacks and the many others carried out by Far East Air Forces planes, so that Corregidor was literally a burnt firecracker by the time our landing forces parachuted down upon it. In the bombardment of Corregidor, two of our B-24s with the crews of Lt. Brown and Lt. Morris were lost operationally flying these missions. Only the co-pilot of Lt. Brown's crew parachuted to safety.'[32]

Opposite page: A stick of bombs dropped by a B-24 of the 494th Bombardment Group explodes on Corregidor during a raid on **14 February 1945**. (NARA)

Above: Daily strikes by USAAF heavy bombers continued from January through until 16 February, with nearly 600 tons of bombs dropped. Estimated figures since the bombing campaign started up to 24 February showed 2,028 effective sorties, with 2,869 tons of bombs dropped on the island.

Here, bombs dropped by the B-24s of the 494th Bombardment Group burst on Corregidor during a raid on **14 February 1945**. (NARA)

Above: A B-24 of the 13th AAF during the attacks on Corregidor. The 'heavy bombers concentrated on gun positions, ammunitions dumps and communication centres'. (US Air Force)

Below: Bombs dropped by the B-24s of the 494th Bombardment Group burst on Corregidor during a raid on **14 February 1945**. Note that ships of the naval task force can be seen arranged in a line across the bottom of the picture, awaiting their turn to bombard Japanese positions on the island. (NARA)

Above: Bombs dropped on Corregidor burst on Topside during a raid on **14 February 1945**, as the preparations for the final assault intensify. (NARA)

Below: B-24s of the 494th Bombardment Group heading back to their base after a mission to attack Caballo and Corregidor islands, **14 February 1945**. (NARA)

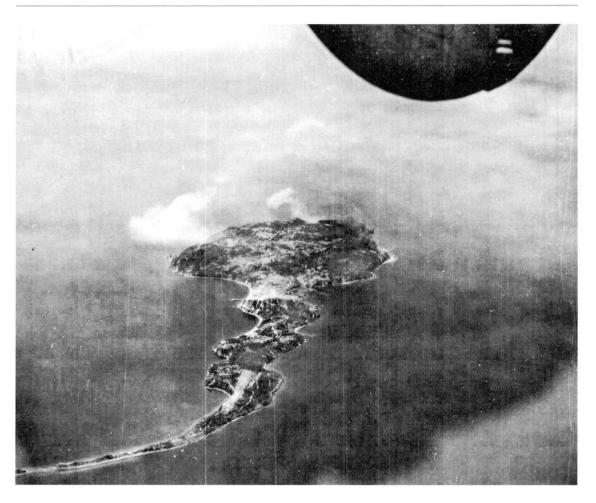

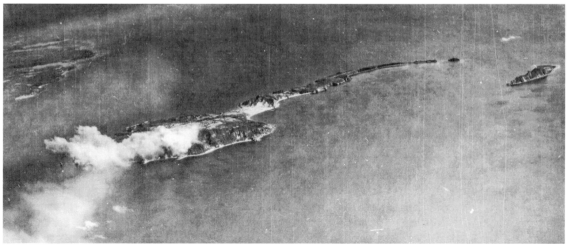

Opposite page top: Bombs dropped by the B-24s of the 494th Bombardment Group burst on the target area on Corregidor during a raid in February 1945. The target in this instance was stated to be 'gun positions on the western end of the island'. (NARA)

Opposite page bottom: Smoke from bombs dropped by the B-24s of the 494th Bombardment Group drifts away from the target area on Corregidor during a raid in February 1945. In this instance, the bombers had been attacking 'gun positions on the western end of the island'. (NARA)

Above: A painting depicting HMAS *Shropshire*, as seen from the destroyer HMAS *Arunta*, firing on Japanese positions on Corregidor. For this mission, *Shropshire* was also accompanied by USS *Portland* (CA-33) and USS *Minneapolis* (CA-36). The following day *Shropshire* was deployed off Luzon in a support role. (Australian War Memorial; ART24226)

Overleaf: Some of the B-24s of the 494th Bombardment Group photographed heading back to their base on **14 February 1945**. (NARA)

Main Image: One of the warships involved in the bombardment of Corregidor was the destroyer USS *Converse II* (DD-509), seen here. Having recently provided fire support for the American landings in Lingayen Gulf on 9 and 10 January 1945, *Converse II* was assigned to the task force allocated to the recapture of Corregidor. During the bombardment her guns 'destroyed gun emplacements, barges, suicide boats, and entombed about 100 enemy troops by sealing the entrance to Malinta Tunnel'. After a brief overhaul in Subic Bay, *Converse II* patrolled off Corregidor until mid-March 1945. (USNHHC)

Above: The north face of Corregidor being bombarded by the Brooklyn-class light cruiser USS *Phoenix* on the morning of **15 February 1945**. The two targets indicated are caves housing Japanese gun positions. (USNHHC)

Below: Cruisers and destroyers of the US Seventh Fleet, which included a number of Royal Australian Navy warships, in action during the bombardment of Corregidor, **15 February 1945**. During the morning of 16 February, cruisers and destroyers blasted the south shore of Bottomside. They also expended considerable ammunition firing on enemy gun positions on Caballo Island and stood by to carry out fire support duties the rest of the day. (Historic Military Press)

Chapter 7

RETURN TO THE ROCK

16–26 February 1945

Planning for the operation to retake Corregidor had begun in earnest on 3 February 1945. The scheme that was quickly formulated called for the principal effort to be an airborne assault supported by a series of nearly simultaneous shore-to-shore amphibious landings. The plans received General MacArthur's approval on 5 February, the date for the assault being set for the 16th.

'The prospective cost of amphibious assault was, indeed, one of the chief factors that led to a decision to use paratroopers,' notes Robert Ross Smith. 'Planners saw the obvious risks in sending parachute troops against such a small and rough target, but in view of the GHQ SWPA [South West Pacific Area – which was commanded by MacArthur] estimate that the Japanese garrison numbered

Below: Two Fletcher-class destroyers, on the left, and a Cleveland-class light cruiser, far right, standing off Corregidor Island as it is bombarded by ships and aircraft on **16 February 1945**, immediately prior to the US landings. The other warship present, second from right, is the force flagship USCGC *Ingham*. (USNHHC)

only 850 men, the cost of the airborne operation promised to be less than that involved in an amphibious attack. [It was] intended to land almost 3,000 troops on Corregidor on 16 February, over 2,000 of them by parachute.

Another 1,000 men or more would come in by parachute or landing craft the next day. Planners hoped that such preponderant strength, combined with intensive air and naval bombardment, might render the seizure of the island nearly bloodless.

'An equally important (if not even more decisive) factor leading to the decision to employ paratroops was the desire to achieve surprise. GHQ SWPA and Sixth Army planners hoped that the Japanese on Corregidor would judge that no one in his right mind would even consider dropping a regiment of parachutists on such a target. The defenses, the planners thought, would probably be oriented entirely toward amphibious attack.'[33]

Following an intense aerial and naval bombardment, the actual task of recapturing Corregidor was handed to a unit that became known as 'Rock Force'. Based around the airborne troops of the 503rd Parachute Regimental Combat Team (PRCT) and the soldiers of the 34th Infantry Regiment, this formation was commanded by Colonel George Madison Jones.

Opposite page: In a final aerial offensive against the Japanese garrison early on the morning of **16 February 1945**, a force of twenty-four B-24s hit known and suspected gun sites, eleven B-25s bombed anti-aircraft gun emplacements and the entire south coast, whilst thirty-one A-20s attacked and strafed assorted positions across Corregidor. Here some of the A-20s are pictured en route to their targets that morning. These aircraft later remained in the area as 'on call' for the ground troops. (NARA)

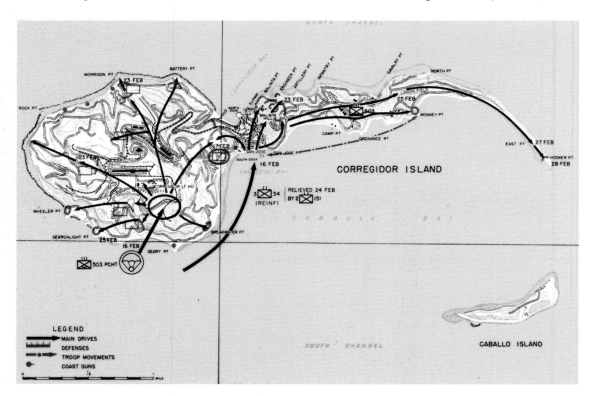

The 503rd Parachute Regimental Combat Team resulted from the activation of the 503rd Parachute Battalion at Fort Benning, Georgia, on 21 August 1941. The battalion was the third of four US Parachute Battalions formed prior to Pearl Harbor. On 5 September 1943, the 503rd jumped in the Markham Valley, New Guinea, marking the first successful airborne combat jump in the Pacific Theatre.

For its part, the 34th Infantry Regiment, commanded by Colonel Aubrey S. 'Red' Newman, was also an experienced unit, having already participated in some of the most horrific combat under the most insufferable weather and terrain of the war so far.

That 'Rock Force' was undoubtedly battle hardened was important for all the evidence and experience gained so far in the Pacific Theatre suggested that the battle to retake Corregidor would be no different from those that preceded it.

Opposite page: The beachhead at San José is attacked by Douglas A-20s at low-level just before the amphibious landings. (NARA)

Below: Two A-20 crew members are rescued from the waters of Manila Bay while Corregidor was being given a pre-invasion bombardment by a US Navy task force which was throwing shells directly over the downed fliers. The Catalina, from the 3rd Emergency Rescue Squadron, had to fly through this and land in heavily mined waters to affect the rescue. The Catalina crew is shown here helping the A-20's pilot, who had suffered a broken nose, jaw and cheekbones, into the flying boat. (NARA)

Above: A view of San José immediately prior to the amphibious landings. Heavy shelling from naval vessels on both sides of the island is underway as barges can be seen approaching under the cover of smoke. (NARA)

Opposite page: 'Parabombs' dropped by Douglas A-20s on Corregidor blow up gun positions and 'keep the Japs undercover just before the arrival of troop planes on invasion day'. (NARA)

Below: Another view of the US amphibious forces heading into shore for the landings at San José. (NARA)

CORREGIDOR

Right: A B-24 Liberator turns away after bombing Corregidor 'on invasion morning' and in so doing, notes the original wartime caption, 'rounds up 25 days of heavy air strikes on this target'. (NARA)

Below: H-Hour nears as US amphibious forces head into shore for the landings at San José on **16 February 1945**. (NARA)

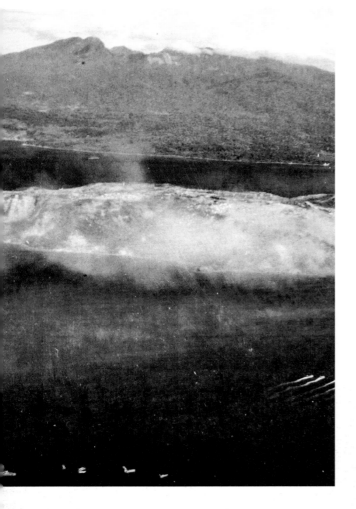

Opposite page top: Douglas C-47s transporting paratroopers to Corregidor, **16 February 1945**. During the planning stages for the operation, Colonel Jones, having undertaken a personal aerial reconnaissance of the island, had initially recommended that Kindley Field would be a suitable drop zone for the paratroopers. This suggestion was overruled, with the area around Topside selected instead. (NARA)

Opposite page bottom: Corregidor as seen from a C-47 approaching 'The Rock' in the final moments before the airborne drops get underway on **16 February 1945**. Almost at the same moment, a force of some seventy A-20s 'bombed and strafed the eastern section of Corregidor and also worked over Caballo'. (NARA)

Below: The airborne landings get underway on **16 February 1945**, as a low-flying Dakota drops its stock of paratroopers 'squarely on target – the shattered bomb-pocket ruin of Corregidor's Top Side'. The first lift that day comprised men of the 3rd Battalion, 503rd Parachute Regimental Combat Team (PRCT), Battery C of the 162nd Parachute Field Artillery Battalion, a platoon of Battery D, 462nd Parachute Field Artillery, Company C of the 161st Airborne Engineer Battalion and assorted headquarters elements. Note that another C-47 can be seen much closer to the ground bottom right. (NARA)

Above: The commander of 'Rock Force', Colonel George Madison Jones. The veteran Harold Templeman once described Jones as 'a West Pointer of the Class of '36' who was 'a pioneer Paratrooper from the days of the original Parachute Battalion'. At the same time, he added, Jones was a 'veteran of two and one-half years in the Pacific', a '33-year-old Commander [who] knew his enemy'. (US Signal Corps)

Above: When Lieutenant Colonel John L. Erickson, the commander of the 503rd's 3rd Battalion, jumped out of a C-47 above Corregidor at about 08.30 hours on **16 February 1945**, he 'stepped into history as the first American paratrooper out the door' in an effort to liberate the island. Once on the ground, Erickson's men were tasked with covering the area of Topside toward the San José beachhead and Malinta Hill. (via Armor Research Library, Fort Benning)

Opposite page: USS *LCS-8* stands off Corregidor's shore to provide fire support as USAAF C-47s (top right) drop paratroopers of the 503rd on the island fortress, **16 February 1945**. (USNHHC)

Above: Paratroopers of the 503rd drop on the parade ground and golf course on Corregidor. The smoke on the right is the result of the naval shelling of the San José area, where the amphibious landings were made. (NARA)

Above: Another view of paratroopers of the 503rd dropping on Topside on Corregidor. Note the other aircraft heading away from the island at a lower altitude. (NARA)

Opposite page: Paratroopers of the 503rd descend on Corregidor, **16 February 1945**. By 09.45 hours all elements of the first lift were on the ground and had assembled at the Topside drop zones. (Library of Congress)

Below: With the pre-invasion bombardment having drawn to a close, smoke still lingers over parts of Topside. With discarded parachutes visible, a C-47 can be seen coming in low over the shore in the middle distance as elements of the naval force stand offshore in the background. (NARA)

Opposite page top: A view of Topside, with the Mile Long Barracks on the far left, taken early on during the airborne landings on **16 February 1945**. (via Armor Research Library, Fort Benning)

Opposite page bottom: Paratroopers from a Douglas C-47 descended on Corregidor during the landings on **16 February 1945**. The historian Ronald Ross Smith states that the 'first man of the first lift of paratroopers was on the ground at 0833 … three minutes behind schedule'. The men of the first lift, he adds, had a number of tasks. They were 'to secure and hold the drop zones for the second lift; prepare to move out to clear all Topside upon the arrival of the second lift; provide fire support for the assault of the 3d Battalion, 34th Infantry, at Bottomside; and, finally, establish physical contact with the latter unit as soon as possible.'[34] (NARA)

Below: It was the crews of the 317th Troop Carrier Group which, flying C-47s, delivered the airborne forces, and their subsequent supplies, to Corregidor. Here the 317th's commander, Colonel John Lackey, briefs his men on a forthcoming mission. Veteran Harold Templeman recalled how 'all the paratroopers were loud in their praise of Colonel Lackey and his troop carrier group who dropped us on the Rock-ribbed citadel. They hit the mark well and they kept on the course, which was no mean job fighting that heavy cross-wind.'[35]

Above: US paratroopers of the 503rd pictured during the drop on **16 February 1945**. It is likely that the building that can just be seen top left is Topside Barracks. (San Diego Air & Space Museum)

Opposite page: Parachutes litter Topside as the drop by the 503rd continues on **16 February 1945**. The first lift had suffered relatively high numbers of casualties, both wounded and killed. Many of the former were the result of the drop, particularly in the early stages, being made at a much higher altitude than planned – 550-600 feet instead of the intended 400 feet – which scattered the men over a much wider area, with many therefore landing in difficult or unsuitable terrain. (NARA)

Above: A member of the 503rd poses for the camera, surrounded by discarded parachutes, on **16 February 1945**. Note the bullet holes on his helmet - both entry and exit - and the blood running down his face. An unexpected consequence of the scattered drop was the death of Captain Akira Itagaki. Concerned at the prospect of the amphibious landings, he had made his way to an observation post near Breakwater Point on the south-east corner of Topside. Whilst there, some thirty US paratroopers landed nearby. Forming up, they quickly attacked the Japanese position and in the ensuing firefight Itagaki was shot and killed. (NARA)

Opposite page: During the morning of **16 February 1945**, a number of the cruisers and destroyers blasted the south shore of Bottomside, where the 3rd Battalion, 34th Infantry, was to land. They then stood by for call fire during the remainder of the day. Here the bombardment of Corregidor that day is pictured from US ships in Manila Bay. (Katherine Hayes Kirkland Collection/USNHHC)

Above: With US paratroopers of the first lift pictured 'in control of Topside', the first wave of landing craft has unloaded at South Dock and all except one boat are on the way out as the second wave comes in. The smoke on the beach is probably from land mines – as the infantry pushed out from south beach, a number of men and vehicles were lost to mines, including a medium tank of the 603rd Tank Company. (NARA)

Above: An aerial view of Corregidor with parachutes in the foreground. Wrecked barracks can be seen in the background. The first four waves of the 34th Infantry put ashore by the landing craft encountered almost no opposition, it was only as the fifth went in that the Japanese defenders began to react. By 11.00 hours, Companies K and L of the 34th Infantry had battled through increasingly stiff opposition to reach the top of Malinta Hill, forcing a wedge through the Japanese garrison. (NARA)

Above: Paratroopers descend on Corregidor during the landings on **16 February 1945**. The second lift began its drop at 12.40 hours, some twenty-five minutes late. It was made up of the 503rd's 2nd Battalion, a battery from the 462nd Parachute Field Artillery Battalion and assorted service and headquarters personnel. (NARA)

Opposite page: With bombs bursting in the foreground, paratroopers can be seen in the background descending on Corregidor during the landings in February 1945. (NARA)

Above: US Navy personnel aboard a 7th Fleet PT boat watch as a raft makes its way to a beach on Corregidor to pick up paratroopers who overshot the top of the island in the airborne assault on **16 February 1945**. (USNHHC)

Opposite page: The raft from the PT boat draws close to the shore of Corregidor whilst recovering mis-dropped paratroopers on **16 February 1945**. (USNHHC)

Below: Discarded parachutes litter Topside in the immediate aftermath of the airborne landings. Note the badly damaged Mile Long Barracks in the background. (NARA)

Above: One member of the 503rd PRCT who jumped on Corregidor on **16 February 1945**, was Private Lloyd G. McCarter, who acted as a scout. Despite the many acts of gallantry and sacrifice displayed on the island over the next few days, McCarter's stood out to such a degree that he was subsequently awarded the Medal of Honor. His citation, dated 10 September 1945, reads as follows:

'Shortly after the initial parachute assault on 16 February 1945, he crossed 30 yards of open ground under intense enemy fire, and at point blank range silenced a machine gun with hand grenades. On the afternoon of 18 February, he killed 6 snipers. That evening, when a large force attempted to bypass his company, he voluntarily moved to an exposed area and opened fire.

'The enemy attacked his position repeatedly throughout the night and was each time repulsed. By 2 o'clock in the morning, all the men about him had been wounded; but shouting encouragement to his comrades and defiance at the enemy, he continued to bear the brunt of the attack, fearlessly exposing himself to locate enemy soldiers and then pouring heavy fire on them. He repeatedly crawled back to the American line to secure more ammunition. When his submachine gun would no longer operate, he seized an automatic rifle and continued to inflict heavy casualties. This weapon, in turn, became too hot to use and, discarding it, he continued with an M-1 rifle.

'At dawn the enemy attacked with renewed intensity. Completely exposing himself to hostile fire, he stood erect to locate the most dangerous enemy positions. He was seriously wounded; but though he had already killed more than 30 of the enemy, he refused to evacuate until he had pointed out immediate objectives for attack. Through his sustained and outstanding heroism in the face of grave and obvious danger, Pvt. McCarter made outstanding contributions to the success of his company and to the recapture of Corregidor.'

The officer who submitted the recommendation for McCarter's award, Lieutenant William Calhoun, later wrote the following of his comrade: 'During April, while we were engaged in combat on [the Philippine island of] Negros, the company was notified that McCarter had been awarded the CMH. We were to take him out of combat immediately if he was with the company, and he was to be given the choice of having the President of the United States present the award in the White House or go to Manila to have the award presented by the commanding general of USAFFE, General MacArthur. Of course, by that time McCarter had been sent back to the States for hospitalization.

'He was discharged in 1945 due to the severity of his wound. He married and lived a quiet life until his wife died due to cancer. In February 1956, while despondent over the death of his wife, and in constant pain because of the bullet which was so close to his heart that it could not be removed, the best warrior I ever knew took his own life.'[36]

Below: An aerial view of the liberation of Corregidor underway on **16 February 1945**. With the paratroopers having gained a foothold on the island, it fell to the men of the 3rd Battalion, 34th Infantry to make the next move. Having set out from Mariveles Harbour at 08.30 hours, their landing craft took a circuitous route around the west end of Corregidor, the first boats hitting the south beach, San José, at 10.28 hours, two minutes ahead of schedule. (NARA)

Above: Bomb damage to buildings on Corregidor's Topside on **16 February 1945**. With Itagaki dead, and the Japanese communication network badly disrupted by the pre-landing bombardment, the defenders, wrote the historian Ronald Ross Smith, soon found themselves 'leaderless' – 'the remaining Japanese were no longer capable of co-ordinated offensive or defensive efforts. Each group would fight on its own from isolated and widely separated strongpoints … operations on Corregidor evolved into a largescale mop-up.'[37] (NARA)

Opposite page: The first American flag to be raised on Corregidor since 1942 is attached by Pfc. Clyde I. Bates and T/5 Frank Guy Arrigo, who climbed 'the tallest remaining pole under Jap sniper fire during [the] first day', **16 February 1945**, to achieve their feat. (via The Armor Research Library, Fort Benning)

Above: Such was the progress of the US operations on the 16th, that further airborne drops planned for the following day were cancelled. The paratroopers were instead transported to the island by landing craft – it was on the afternoon of the 17th, for example, that the men of the 503rd's 1st Battalion were put ashore at Bottomside with other reinforcements. The transports therefore limited themselves to resupply drops – as in the case of this C-47 pictured over Corregidor on **17 February 1945**. (via Armor Research Library, Fort Benning)

Opposite page: Un-coordinated and disjointed though it may have been, the Japanese defence on Corregidor was typically dogged and ferocious. As the paratroopers and infantry fought to clear the enemy from their positions, both above and below ground, they frequently faced a defiant foe.

In this image, an American soldier is pictured deploying a bazooka against a Japanese position as Rock Force's operations to liberate Corregidor continue – note the abandoned parachute hanging over him. Veteran Harold Templeman noted the following: 'Firing bazookas point blank into the openings, the assault teams moved in, screening themselves with white phosphorous grenades until the flame throwers could fire their death-dealing blasts into the entrances. Japs came screaming from their hideouts in flames to be mowed down by the supporting Infantrymen ... The systematic destruction of the enemy followed the same pattern so effective the first day with bazookas, white phosphorous, flame throwers, and demolitions supported by Infantry and Artillery. By the end of the third day, more than a thousand Japs had been flushed from their caves and killed.'[38] (Historic Military Press)

Above: As the Americans continued to re-establish themselves on Corregidor and gradually reduce any remaining pockets of resistance, during the night of **23 February 1945**, Japanese soldiers trapped inside the Malinta tunnels as a result of the shelling by USS *Converse II* proceeded to detonate ammunition or explosives deep inside the hill – this photograph show the front view of one of the lateral tunnels in the Malinta complex. 'In the early morning hours,' notes one account, 'seven explosions, all in quick succession, threatened to tear the hill asunder. Foxholes crumbled, flames belched from every hole in the central and northern portions of the hill, and with it belched corpses blown out by the blast, and men driven out into American fire and death. It was devastation – stark, awe inspiring, terrifying.' The collapsed laterals resulting from these explosions have never been excavated. (NARA)

Opposite page: By the end of **24 February 1945**, the men of Rock Force were in possession of all but the last 3,000 or so yards of Corregidor's 'tail'; the following day, despite stiff resistance by isolated groups of Japanese defenders and the continual threat of banzai charges, this had been compressed even further to just 1,000 yards. By the 28th, the liberators finally reached Hooker Point at the far end of the 'tail'. Photographed by a cameraman aboard a Consolidated B-24 Liberator this is the recaptured garrison area on Topside. The 'bomb-gutted buildings and craters testify to the effectiveness of the air strikes' undertaken in advance of the landings. (NARA)

Above: As the original caption states, 'like gaunt and blackened eyes, the ruins of Corregidor looked up … after the Fifth Air Force had battered it'. This is another view of the battle-scarred Mile Long Barracks.

Shortly after 11.00 hours on **26 February 1945**, the Japanese on Corregidor executed their 'final, suicidal tour de force' by blowing up an underground arsenal at Monkey Point near the island's 'tail'. Four smaller explosions followed, and a ravine was created where a hill had formerly existed. The blast was, recalled Harold Templeman, 'of the greatest intensity yet experienced and the "Rock" shook and shuddered to its very foundations deep in the sea'.

Such was the scale of the explosion, that lumps of rock landed over a mile away at Topside or fell on ships some 2,000 yards offshore. A US medium tank was thrown through the air, killing most of its crew. Over 200 Japanese died in the blast, whilst some fifty US personnel lost their lives and a further 150 were wounded. Devastating though the incident was, it did mark the last act of organised Japanese resistance on Corregidor. (NARA)

Chapter 8

AFTERMATH

The ending of organised Japanese resistance on 26 February 1945, by no means marked the end of the campaign to liberate Corregidor. Over the days that followed, the difficult task of prising small groups or individual enemy stragglers, or 'holdouts' as they were commonly known, from their camouflaged foxholes, caves and tunnels continued.

Above: By **1 March 1945**, the devastated island bastion was officially opened to Allied shipping. Here, Vice Admiral Daniel E. Barbey, Seventh Fleet (in the centre), sets out in a Jeep for an inspection of Corregidor the following day. (USNHHC)

Opposite page top: American troops 'mopping up' remaining Japanese resistance in the caves and tunnels on Corregidor.

As late as 1 January 1946, a lone soldier serving in an American Graves Registration Unit was busy recording newly erected grave markers when he suddenly encountered some twenty Japanese soldiers who approached him waving an improvised white flag. The 'holdouts' had been sheltering in a tunnel or cave on Corregidor. They only discovered that Japan had surrendered when one of the group, who had ventured out in search of water and food, came across a newspaper that mentioned their country's defeat. (US Army)

Opposite page bottom: General MacArthur on board a US Navy PT boat, more specifically *PT-373*, arriving at one of the wrecked docks at Corregidor on **2 March 1945**. Standing to his left is Brigadier General Carlos P. Romulo, commanding General of the Philippine Forces of Liberation.

Commanded by Lieutenant Belton A. Copp, during the night of 7 February 1945, *PT-373* was the first US Navy vessel, of a two-boat squadron, to enter Manila Harbor since the retreat in 1942. It did so as part of a night reconnaissance undertaken 'in order to test defenses'. General McArthur duly honoured Copp and his crew by using their boat to transport him back into Manila Harbor on 2 March 1945. (NARA)

Below: General MacArthur picks his way through the rubble on the battered island of Corregidor following his return in March 1945. During his tour of the island on **2 March 1945**, MacArthur headed to Topside and inspected his former office, finding it badly damaged. It is also said that he visited his old accommodation to see if a case of Scotch he had buried under the steps was still there! (NARA)

Above: Colonel George M. Jones pictured on Corregidor studying a plaque commemorating Samuel M. Mills, after whom Fort Mills, the official term for the military defences on the island, was named. For his leadership of Rock Force, Jones was awarded the Distinguished Service Cross, the medal being presented by MacArthur during the ceremonies on Topside on **2 March 1945**.

By 2 March 1945, it was reported that Allied casualties, including those from the parachute drops, numbered over 1,000 killed, wounded or injured, and missing. The figures on the Japanese side were much higher, for their losses, at least those that could be counted, amounted to some 4,500 killed. Just twenty or so of the enemy garrison were captured alive. It was also thought that at least 500 might have been sealed in the myriad caves and tunnels on the island – though the true figure will never be known.

An additional 200 Japanese were estimated to have been killed or drowned while trying to swim away from Corregidor, in particular north towards the Bataan Peninsula or south to nearby Caballo Island. 'They were straffed by planes,' noted Harold Templeman, 'picked up by PT boats and engineer supply boats, or found by American troops waiting for them on the shores of Bataan peninsula. Lt. Thomas, our artillery observation pilot, took part in this strafing, using a Tommy-gun from his open-cabin plane.'[39]

It was also on 2 March that Colonel Jones and General Charles Philip Hall, the commanding officer of XI Corps, felt able to officially declare the end of the Corregidor operation. With this, Rock Force ceased to exist, the various units involved reverting to their normal chain of command.

At about 10.00 hours on 2 March 1945, a PT boat idled up to the shoreline at San José. On board was General MacArthur, returning just three days short of three years since his departure. He was welcomed back to 'The Rock' by Colonel Jones. Men from all the units that had comprised Rock Force, including a platoon from 3rd Battalion, 34th Infantry, which returned from Mariveles, to where they had been withdrawn a few days earlier, were formed up as an Honour Guard for the General to inspect.

Below: On setting foot on Corregidor, MacArthur made the following statement: 'I see that the old flagpole still stands. Have your troops hoist the colors to its peak and let no enemy ever again haul it down.' Veteran Harold Templeman later described what followed: 'Climaxing a fortnight of bitter fighting, Corporal Donald G. Bauer, a 503rd Paratrooper from Dayton, Ohio, hauled to the top of a bomb and shell scarred mast, the Stars and Stripes. In a short, simple, but impressive ceremony, the Fortress Corregidor officially became once more American territory after being held for nearly three years by the Japanese.'[41] (NARA)

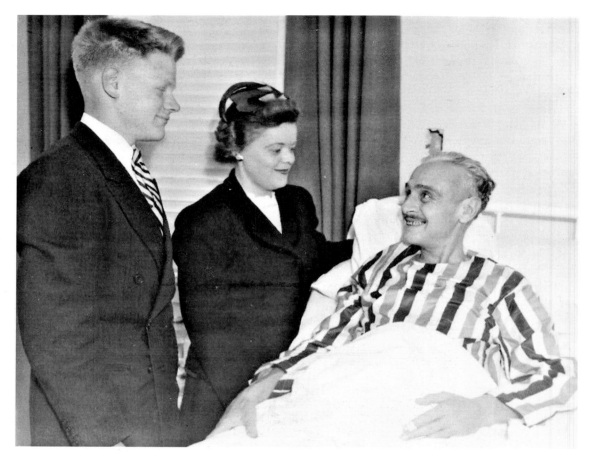

Above: Following his release from a Japanese PoW camp, Lieutenant Colonel Frank F. Carpenter is reunited with his wife and son in a hospital in California on **3 March 1945**. A member of MacArthur's staff, Carpenter remained on Corregidor after the General's departure and was captured following the garrison's surrender. He was subsequently held in various camps in the Philippines, including Bilibid Prison. (Historic Military Press)

One officer of the 503rd later recalled in his journal what happened next: 'Almost all the men of the regiment with the exception of the honor guard were placed at intervals of about ten feet along both sides of the road from Topside to Bottomside to protect General MacArthur and his party …

'After the General landed at the North Dock, which was protected by a .50 caliber machine gun section under 1st Lt Charlie Horton, C Battery, he insisted on walking several feet into the east entrance of Malinta Tunnel. He stood there for a couple of minutes peering into the dark interior of the tunnel. Everyone held their breath expecting to hear a shot, or shots, ring out from the depths of the tunnel. The General casually walked back to the waiting entourage standing beside their Jeeps. The convoy proceeded up the road to Topside between the two lines of troops.'[40]

'The cavalcade of Jeeps bearing the dignitaries,' recalled Harold Templeman in taking up the story, 'pulled up to one corner of the old Parade Grounds where bulldozers had hastily leveled off an area for the flag-raising ceremonies. In the center of the area stood the flag pole, a slightly-bent, shell and bomb scarred ship's mast with twisted rigging and ladders still hanging from its yardarm. In the background white and camouflage parachutes dangled from the trees and wrecked buildings. Bright colored equipment canopies flapped in the breeze where they hung, their cargoes of guns and ammunition hurriedly cut from their lines two weeks before.'

During the simple, yet impressive flag-raising ceremony on the parade ground at Topside that followed, Colonel Jones stepped forward, saluted MacArthur, and reported: 'Sir, I present to you Fortress Corregidor.' In his reply, MacArthur stated: 'Colonel Jones, the capture of Corregidor is one of the most brilliant operations in military history. Outnumbered two to one, your command by its unfaltering courage, its invincible determination, and its professional skill overcame all obstacles and annihilated the enemy.'

MacArthur also announced that he was recommending a Presidential Citation for Rock Force. The citation, when duly confirmed, ended with the following statement: 'Throughout the operation all elements of the task force, combat and service troops alike, displayed heroism in the highest degree. Parachuting to earth or landing on the mined beaches, they attacked savagely against a numerically superior enemy, defeated him completely, and. seized the fortress. Their magnificent courage, tenacity, and gallantry avenged the victims of Corregidor of 1942 and achieved a significant victory for the United States Army.'

Below: A view of Corregidor after its recapture. The last of the main Japanese defence was confined to the 'tail', seen here to the left. This image was taken on **11 July 1945**. (NARA)

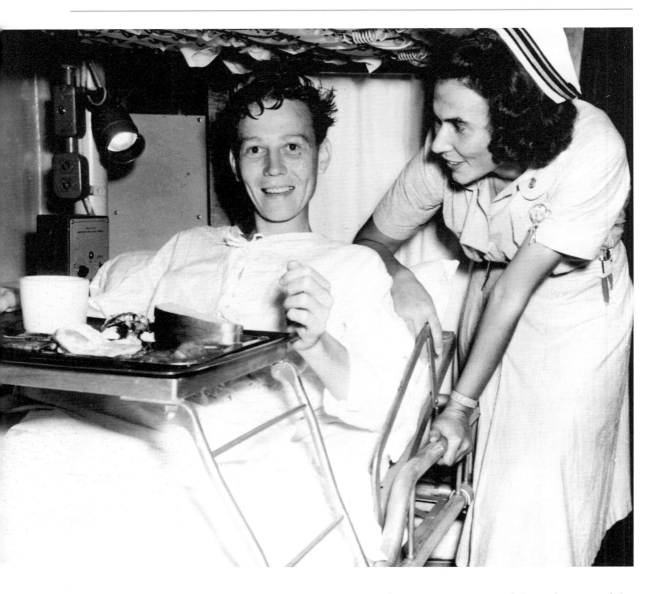

Above: Alfred Sorenson, a released US Army prisoner of war, contemplates a full meal in one of the wards on the hospital ship USS *Benevolence* on **30 August 1945**. Sorenson had been captured at Corregidor on 6 May 1942. He was eventually liberated from a prisoner of war camp near Tokyo. (USNHHC)

Opposite page: Liberated prisoners of war at Bilibid Prison pictured after their liberation by a US tank destroyer unit in February 1945. All five are stated to have been originally captured on Corregidor and are showing the effect of their incarceration. Left to right, they are Pfc Edward B. Claypool (E Company, 2nd Battalion, 4th Marine Regiment); Sergeant David W. Brumfield; Pfc Fred Dunn; Pharmacist's Mate Thomas F. Brannon Jr.; and Captain Fred G. Nasr. The latter two are holding 'bottles containing the daily diet the men were subjected to', and which provided 600 calories or less.

Just how long some families had to wait for news of the fate of their loved ones after the fall of Corregidor is illustrated by the following article that appeared in the Arkansas newspaper *Hope Star*, in their edition of 27 February 1943. It finally gave news of Brumfield's capture: 'Sergeant David W. Brumfield, son of Mr and Mrs Thomas H. Brumfield of Hope, who has been missing since the fall of Corregidor to the Japanese, is a Japanese prisoner in the Philippines, the War Department notified his parents here today by telegram. Sergeant Brumfield, an army veteran, saw service in the Philippines several years prior to the outbreak of war.

'He was in action throughout the campaign on Bataan peninsula and later on Corregidor fortress. Shortly after Corregidor capitulated to the Japanese he was officially listed as missing by the War Department.' (NARA)

Above: General Douglas MacArthur and Lieutenant General Jonathan Wainwright greet each other at the New Grand Hotel at Yokohama, Japan, on **31 August 1945**. It was their first meeting since they had parted on Corregidor more than three years before. Wainwright, always a tall, thin individual, hence his nickname of 'Skinny', was even thinner and malnourished after three years of captivity. He was the highest-ranking American PoW of the Second World War. (United States Defense Visual Information Center)

Opposite page: As he makes his way home, Chief Yeoman Edwin D. Williams USN, another Corregidor veteran and prisoner of war, is pictured on board USS *Rescue* on **7 September 1945**. He was captured on 6 May 1942, spending three years and three months in enemy prison camps. (National Museum of the US Navy)

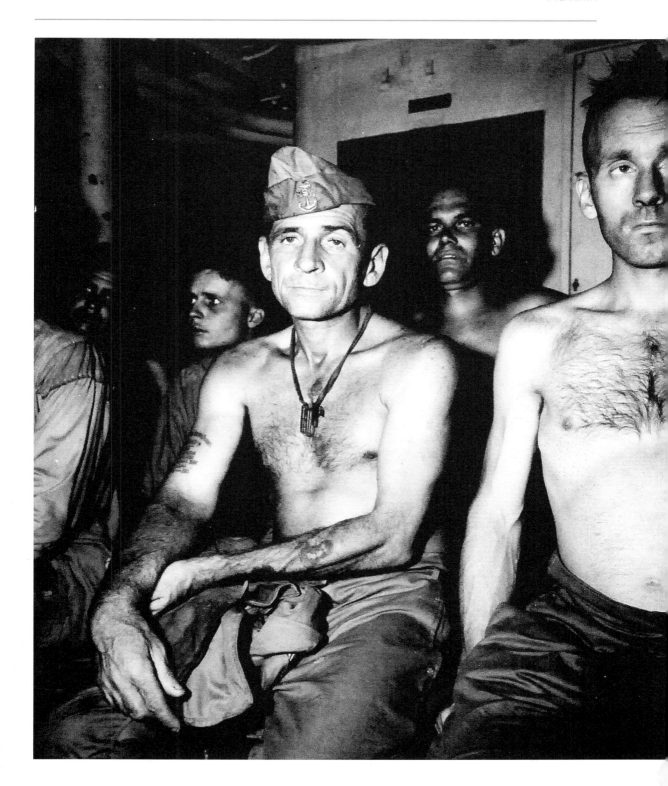

Right: Another group of liberated prisoners of war. The five men, all of whom are saluting, were, according to the original caption, captured on Corregidor. They are, left to right, Pfc William Sutherland, Petty Officer 3rd Class E.M. Burnett, Sergeant David A. Granger (on crutches), Corporal Edward Hayden and Pfc James Morris. The picture was taken at the airfield at Atsugi, near the cities of Yamato and Ayase in Kanagawa Prefecture, Japan. (NARA)

Above: A US Army Chaplain, Major Albert W. Braun, conducts a service aboard a US Navy aircraft carrier during his repatriation to the United States in September 1945. Major Braun was captured by the Japanese at Corregidor, though he was allowed to continue to conduct services, for which local Filipinos helped him obtain altar supplies. (National Museum of the US Navy)

Right: On 5 September 1945, it was proposed that General Jonathan Mayhew 'Skinny' Wainwright IV should be awarded the Medal of Honor for his actions on Corregidor in 1942. President Truman promptly approved the recommendation. The subsequent citation, dated **19 September 1945**, states that Wainwright, seen here at the time of his investiture, 'Distinguished himself by intrepid and determined leadership against greatly superior enemy forces. At the repeated risk of life above and beyond the call of duty in his position, he frequented the firing line of his troops where his presence provided the example and incentive that helped make the gallant efforts of these men possible.

'The final stand on beleaguered Corregidor, for which he was in an important measure personally responsible, commanded the admiration of the Nation's allies. It reflected the high morale of American arms in the face of overwhelming odds. His courage and resolution were a vitally needed inspiration to the then sorely pressed freedom-loving peoples of the world.'

This was not the first time, however, that Wainwright had been put forward for such an award, as one author points out: 'On July 30, 1942 General George C. Marshall proposed that a Medal of Honor be awarded to the last of the fighting generals. It prompted an act of resistance to a Medal of Honor award unprecedented in the Medal's history.

'General MacArthur wrote, in part: "The citation proposed does not represent the truth. As a relative matter award of the Medal of Honor to General Wainwright would be a grave injustice to a number of general officers of practically equally responsible positions who not only distinguished themselves by fully as great personal gallantry thereby earning the DSC but exhibited powers of leadership and inspiration to a degree greatly superior to that of General Wainwright thereby contributing much more to the stability of the command and to the successful conduct of the campaign. It would be a grave mistake, which later on might well lead to embarrassing repercussions to make this award." MacArthur's vehement opposition to Wainwright's proposed award both surprised and stunned General Marshall. He withdrew the recommendation.'[42]

MacArthur did not oppose the award in 1945. (US War Department)

Opposite page: US servicemen inspect bomb or shell damage on Corregidor on **16 September 1945**. (NARA)

Above: A group of veterans, who have gathered behind a sign reading 'Survivors of Bataan and Corregidor Death March!', prepare to participate in a parade after the end of the war. (USNHHC)

Opposite page: Rear Admiral John D. Bulkeley inspects a 12-inch mortar battery during his tour of Corregidor Island. The photograph, taken by Journalist First Class W.G. Broome, is dated **8 August 1977**. This mortar is one of four such weapons that were located at Battery Way. (USNHHC)

Right: Rear Admiral John D. Bulkeley reads the commemorative sign by the entrance to Malinta Tunnel. The inscription states: 'General Douglas MacAarthur had his headquarters here from December 30, 1941 to March 12, 1942. Here too the Government of the Commonwealth was transferred on December 24, 1941. At the West Entrance on Rizal Day, Manuel L. Quezon and Sergid Osmeña took their oath of office for their second term as President and Vice-President, respectively, of the Philippines. Near the East Entrance on May 6, 1942 the defenders of Corregidor made their desperate stand.' (USNHHC)

Above: Rear Admiral John D. Bulkeley peers down the barrel of a surviving US 12-inch Mortar, No.172, during his return to Corregidor island in 1977. (USNHHC)

Left: Rear Admiral John D. Bulkeley, the President of the US Navy Board of Inspection and Survey, points out the old North Pier on Corregidor to Lieutenant Commander Erwin Sharp USN during his return to the island in August 1977. It was from this very spot that Bulkeley, then in charge of *PT-41* (see Chapter 2), evacuated General MacArthur, members of his family, and other senior officers, on the night of 11-12 March 1942. (USNHHC)

Below: During his visit to Corregidor in August 1977, Rear Admiral John D. Bulkeley took a moment to honour the fallen, saluting the Corregidor Monument after placing a wreath on it. (USNHHC)

Below: Evidence of the battering endured by Corregidor is still starkly visible to this day. The structure seen here, the exposed Middleside Barracks, was devastated in the early bombing. (John Grehan)

Above: Another photograph showing the ruins of Middleside Barracks, providing further evidence of the bombardment that Corregidor endured. (John Grehan)

Above: Another view of the ruins of Middleside Barracks which were abandoned by the Japanese and never rebuilt or repaired. (John Grehan)

Above: The ruins of Mile Long Barracks on Corregidor's Topside. This building is claimed to be the longest barracks in the world, hence the name. (John Grehan)

Opposite page: Remains of the thirteen-and-a-half miles of railway track for the electric train which ran around Fort Mills on Corregidor, and which was largely destroyed by the Japanese bombing and shelling. (John Grehan)

Right: The memorial to Rock Force that can be seen adjacent to the parade ground on Topside. (NARA)

Overleaf: The Brothers in Arms Statue, the American-Filipino memorial on Topside, Corregidor, with the ruins of the former cinema behind. Inaugurated in 1968, it was the first American memorial on Philippine soil since the United States had recognized the country as an independent nation in 1946. (John Grehan)

IN THESE HALLOWED SURROUNDINGS WHERE
HAD THEIR ASHES SCATTER WITH THE WIND AND L...
THOSE WHO WERE LEFT BEHIND
THEY DIED FOR FREEDOM'S RIGHT AND IN HE...
THEIRS WAS A NOBLE CAUSE

NOTES AND REFERENCES

1. Formed in 1941, the Far East Air Force (FEAF) was the military aviation organization of the US Army in the Philippines. After the Japanese successes in the Pacific following Pearl Harbor, the surviving elements of FEAF were withdrawn to Australia where, on 5 February 1942, they were redesignated the 5th Air Force.
2. Louis Morton, *The Fall of the Philippines* (Center of Military History, US Army, Washington D.C., 1952), p.129.
3. Quoted in Greenberger, Robert, *The Bataan Death March: World War II Prisoners in the Pacific* (Compass Point Books, Minneapolis, 2009), p.96.
4. See Eric Morris, *Corregidor: The American Alamo of World War II* (Cooper Square Press, New York, 1981).
5. Louis Morton, 'Bataan Diary of Major Achille C. Tisdelle', *Military Affairs* Vol.11, No.3 (Autumn, 1947), pp.130-148.
6. William Bartsch, 'Corregidor', *After the Battle*, No.23, 1979, pp.1-28.
7. Louis Morton, *The Fall of the Philippines, op. cit*, pp.493-4.
8. From the diary of Major Achille C. Tisdelle, quoted in ibid, p.494.
9. Richard Connaughton, *MacArthur and Defeat in the Philippines* (Overlook Press, Woodstock, 2001), p.224.
10. See Dr Edward C. Whitman, 'Submarines to Corregidor', *Undersea Warfare* magazine, Issue 15.
11. ibid.
12. Hiroshi Masuda, *MacArthur in Asia: The General and His Staff in the Philippines, Japan and Korea* (Cornell University Press, 2013).
13. Frazier Hunt, *The Untold Story of Douglas MacArthur* (Devin-Adair, New York, 1954).
14. Richard Connaughton, p.288.
15. William Manchester, *American Caesar: Douglas MacArthur, 1880-1964* (Hutchinson, New York, 1978), p.290.
16. General Douglas MacArthur, Reminiscences (McGraw Hill, New York, 1964), p.142.
17. Dr Edward C. Whitman, 'Submarines to Corregidor', *op. cit*.
18. Quoted in Louis Morton, *The Fall of the Philippines*, pp.542-3.
19. James H. Belote and William M. Belote, *Corregidor, The Stirring Saga of a Fortress* (Playboy Press, New York, 1967), pp.130-1.
20. Bill Sloan, *Undefeated, America's Heroic Fight for Bataan and Corregidor* (Simon & Schuster, New York, 2012), p.208.
21. Recollections of Captain Ann Bernatitus NC, USN, (Retd.), quoted on www.history.navy.mil.
22. Louis Morton, *The Fall of the Philippines, op. cit.*, p.541.
23. See Leon M. Guerrero, 'The Last Days of Corregidor', *The Philippine Review*, May 1943.
24. Quoted at the excellent website www.corregidor.org/USMC.

NOTES AND REFERENCES

25. Kazumaro Uno, *Corregidor: Isle of Delusion* (Press Bureau, Imperial Japanese Army, GHQ, China, September 1942), p.19.
26. Quoted in Baldwin, 'The Fourth Marines at Corregidor,' Part III, *Marine Corps Gazette* (January 1947), p.24.
27. Louis Morton, *The Fall of the Philippines*, *op. cit.*, p.560.
28. Hough, Lieutenant Colonel Frank O., USMCR, Ludwig, Major Verle E., USMC, and Shaw, Henry I. Jr., *Pearl Harbor to Guadalcanal – History of U.S. Marine Corps Operations in World War II*, Vol. I, (USMC, undated), p.200.
29. Quoted from the informative website www.navsource.org/archives/11/02015.htm.
30. Robert Ross Smith, *The War in the Pacific: Triumph in the Philippines* (Department of the Army, Washington, 1963), p.339.
31. ibid.
32. Quoted from *History of the 494th Bomb Group (H)*, published by The 494th Bomb Group (H) Association, Inc.
33. Robert Ross Smith, p.341.
34. ibid.
35. Harold Templeman, *The Return to Corregidor* (Strand Press, New York).
36. Calhoun's full account can be seen at: www.corregidor.org/heritage_battalion/moh/mccarter_calhoun.html
37. Robert Ross Smith, p.345.
38. Harold Templeman, *The Return to Corregidor*.
39. ibid.
40. Quoted in the history of the 2/503 Parachute Infantry Regiment at www.corregidor.org.
41. Harold Templeman, *The Return to Corregidor*.
42. For more information see 'Family Feud: A Tale of Two Generals' at www.homeofheroes.com.

SELECT BIBLIOGRAPHY

Berhow, Mark A. and McGovern, Terrance C., *American Defenses of Corregidor and Manila Bay 1898–1945* (Osprey Publishing, Oxford, 2003)

Belote, James H. and Belote, William M., *Corregidor: The Stirring Saga of a Mighty Fortress* (Playboy Press, New York, 1980)

Connaughton, Richard, *MacArthur and Defeat in the Philippines* (Overlook Press, New York, 2001)

Hough, Lieutenant Colonel Frank O., USMCR, Ludwig, Major Verle E., USMC, and Shaw, Henry I. Jr., *Pearl Harbor to Guadalcanal – History of U.S. Marine Corps Operations in World War II*, Vol. I, (USMC, undated)

MacArthur, General Douglas, *Reminiscences* (McGraw Hill, New York, 1964)

Masuda, Hiroshi, *MacArthur in Asia: The General and His Staff in the Philippines, Japan and Korea* (Cornell University Press, 2013)

Morris, Eric, *Corregidor: The American Alamo of World War II* (Cooper Square Press, New York, 1981)

Morton, Louis, *The Fall of the Philippines* (Center of Military History, US Army, Washington D.C., 1952)

Sloan, Bill, *Undefeated: America's Heroic Fight for Bataan and Corregidor* (Simon & Schuster, New York, 2012)

Smith, Robert Ross, *The War in the Pacific: Triumph in the Philippines* (Department of the Army, Washington, 1963)

Templeman, Harold, *The Return to Corregidor* (Strand Press, New York, undated)

Waldron, Ben, and Burneson, Emily, *Corregidor: From Paradise to Hell!* (Trafford Publishing, New York, 2003)

Whitcomb, Edgar D., *Escape From Corregidor* (Henry Regnery Company, Chicago, 1958)